Three Abecedaria

With best wishes,

Jerry

Three Abecedaria

An Alphabetical Approach to Vocabulary

by Jeremiah Reedy

Bolchazy-Carducci Publishers, Inc.
Mundelein, Illinois USA

Editor: Connor Hart
Contributing Editor: Laurel Draper
Design & Layout: Adam Phillip Velez
Cover Graphic & Illustrations: Mary Ann Reedy

Three Abecedaria
An Alphabetical Approach to Vocabulary

Jeremiah Reedy

Bolchazy-Carducci Publishers, Inc.
1570 Baskin Road
Mundelein, Illinois 60060
www.bolchazy.com

Printed in the United States of America
2018
by Publishers' Graphics

ISBN 978-0-86516-856-5

Library of Congress Cataloging-in-Publication Data

Names: Reedy, Jeremiah, author.
Title: Three abecedaria : an alphabetical approach to vocabulary / by
  Jeremiah Reedy.
Description: Mundelein, Illinois, USA : Bolchazy-Carducci Publishers, Inc.,
  2018. | Includes bibliographical references and index.
Identifiers: LCCN 2018022196 | ISBN 9780865168565 (pbk.)
Subjects: LCSH: English language--Foreign elements--Greek--Dictionaries. |
  English language--Foreign elements--Latin--Dictionaries.
Classification: LCC PE1582.G6 R44 2018 | DDC 422/.481--dc23

In memory of Grace L. Beede,
Teacher, Mentor, and Colleague

Contents

Introduction

ABECEDARIA is the plural of the word ABECEDARIUM (also ABECE-DARIAN), which is a book consisting of words arranged alphabetically. Most abecedaria are for small children—"A is for apple; B is for ball; C is for cat," etc. The abecedaria that make up this book are for high school students, especially juniors and seniors, who may want to increase their vocabularies before going to college or out into the world of work. As far as the author knows, this is the first book of this type to have been written explicitly for high school students. The first section consists of English words derived from Greek, the second section deals with English words derived from Latin, and the third section with Latin phrases that are sometimes found in English. Words in each section are broken down into their constituent parts (prefixes, suffixes, and roots), and then the meaning of each element is discussed. The hope is that readers will learn to do this by themselves. A further hope is that some who use this book and see the contributions that Latin and Greek have made to English may be motivated to study the classical languages themselves. Ultimately the purpose of this book is to turn readers into logophiles or philologists, i.e., "lovers of words."

It is commonly known that most of our English words come from Latin, Greek, and Anglo-Saxon. These languages belong to the Indo-European family of languages and scholars in the field known as comparative grammar have been able to reconstruct hundreds and hundreds of roots that belonged to Proto-Indo-European (PIE hereafter), the prehistoric language from which the Indo-European languages are derived. (In linguistics "roots" are the basic elements of words that carry the meaning and to which prefixes and suffixes are added.) These roots, together with an excellent article by Calvert Watkins, can be found at the back of the *American Heritage*

Dictionary of the English Language. Watkins describes "the comparative method," gives examples of reconstructed roots, and discusses what can be said about the culture of the speakers of PIE based on these roots. This includes, for example, their economic life, their technology, and their ideology. People find this absolutely fascinating since the speakers of PIE spoke a language that is ancestral to English. I am presenting here a simplified chart that shows the relationship that exists between the languages of this family. When relevant, PIE roots are discussed under individual letters. It is the author's conviction that many insights and fascinating bits of knowledge that cannot be found elsewhere can be found in the etymology (i.e., the origin) of our words.

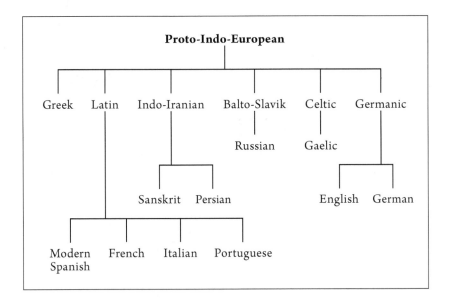

Etymology is the study of the origin of words. The etymology of etymology is this: *etym-* is from Greek *etymon*, which means "true"; *-o-* is used to join the parts of many compound words, and *-logy* means "study of." Etymology should therefore mean "the study of the true meaning of words," though the current meaning of a word may be quite different from the original meaning, as we shall often see in this book. Nevertheless, knowing the original meaning of a word is very important for aspiring logophiles, and often very interesting, as we shall also see. There are some people (such as myself) who would like to know the etymology of every word in the English language! This is both a blessing and a curse, like many things in life.

Since there are twenty-six letters in our alphabet, one might expect there to be seventy-eight units in these three abecedaria. There are, however, only sixty-six. This is because the Greek alphabet in antiquity had only twenty-four letters, lacking as it did letters with sounds corresponding to *c, f, j, q, v, w, x,* and *y,* but it contained some we do not have, namely *th* (*theta*), *ph* (*phi*), *ch* (*chi*), long *e* (*eta*), and long *o* (*omega*). *Nota bene:* The Greek letter *k* (*kappa*) frequently shows up in English as *c.* Their alphabet did not contain the letter *f;* hence there are no English words that begin with *f* that are derived from Greek. Greek did, however, have words that begin with *ph-.* They will be discussed after words beginning with *p.*

The Roman alphabet was very similar to ours, but they did not have *w.* Also *x, y,* and *z* were only used to spell words borrowed from Greek. According to *Lewis and Short, z* came into use in Cicero's day (106–43 BCE) but only to represent *zeta* in words borrowed from Greek. No native Latin words have a *z* in them. Hence the sixty-six units of this book. Thus during the summer before going to college a student who is pressed for time could do one unit per day and be done in slightly over two months. Obviously one who has more time to devote to vocabulary building could complete the book in a much shorter time. The author recommends writing prefixes, suffixes, and roots on cards and repeating them until they have been committed to memory. The student who does this will be in a position to figure out many more words than the ones covered in this book.

There have been many people who not only loved words but could be said to have been crazy about them. Pablo Neruda, the Chilean writer, wrote,

> I run after certain words . . . They are so beautiful that I want to fit them all into my poem . . . I catch them in mid-flight, as they buzz past, I trap them, clean them, peel them, I set myself in front of the dish, they have a crystalline texture to

me, vibrant, ivory, vegetable, oily, like fruit, like algae, like
agates, like olives . . . And then I stir them, I shake them,
I let them go . . . they have shadow, transparence, weight,
feathers, hair, and everything they gathered from so much
rolling down the river, from so much wandering from country to country, from being roots so long . . . They are very
ancient and very new.[1]

   W. H. Auden, another poet, was once asked what advice he would
give an aspiring poet. Auden said that he would ask why the person
wants to write: "If the answer was 'Because I have something terribly
important to say' . . . there could be small hope of expecting poetry
from him. If, on the other hand, the answer was 'Because I like to
hang around words and overhear them whisper to one another,' then
that man might fail of any of thousands of human reasons but he had
a poet's interest in the poem and could be hoped for."[2]
   One of the purposes of this book is to persuade students that,
although they may have no desire to write poetry, they should nevertheless "hang around words and overhear them whisper to one
another."
   Charles Ferguson, senior editor of *Readers' Digest* for many years,
wrote that a word "should be treated as an entity, as an Emersonian
person so real it will bleed, as a world that sums up eons of life, a
thing in itself, not a blob on a page or a noise in the ear. A word is to
be seen as history marvelously compressed, as a distillate of human
experience because it has had human experience passing in and out
of minds and across tongues in countless situations, witnessing and
savoring what has gone on in its presence and by means of it."[3]

---

1   Pablo Neruda, *Memoirs*, trans. Hardie St. Martin (New York: Farrar, Straus and
     Giroux, 1977), 53–54.

2   Quoted by John Ciardi, "Manner of Speaking," *Saturday Review* 55, March 11,
     1972, 14.

3   Personal letter to the author.

Words come with retinues of associations and connotations.[4] They have textures, shapes, tastes, and histories. Words have particular demands on the speech muscles. According to George Steiner, words have "angularities," "concavities," "forces of tectonic suggestion," and "rugosity" (wrinkles); for some poets words even have distinctive smells.[5] Homer speaks of "wooly" screams, Dante of "hairy" and "shaggy" words, and also of "combed out," "glossy," and "rumpled" ones.

The purpose of this book is not simply to impart to students the knowledge of prefixes, suffixes, and roots, laudable as that goal is, nor do I expect many to begin trapping words as they buzz by or to begin smelling words or listening to them "whisper to one another." The larger purpose of this book is to equip readers to become logophiles or philologists and explore for themselves the histories and connotations of the words they encounter.

---

4   A version of this paragraph was previously published in Jeremiah Reedy, "It's a Factoid, Tessa's in Italy, Latin Is Asset in Which the Author Discusses 101 Ways to Enliven a Course in Vocabulary Building," *Classical Journal* 76, no. 3 (February–March 1981): 259–265.

5   George Steiner, *After Babel* (Oxford: Oxford University Press, 1975), 292–293.

Words Derived from Greek

A is for Apocalypticism.

The prefix *apo-* can mean "away from," "without," and "not," *inter alia* ("among other things"), but in APOCALYPTICISM, *apo-* indicates "reversal." *Calypt-* has to do with covering or concealing; hence *apocalypt-* means "uncover." The suffix *-ic* means "of" or "relating to" and *-ism* means "doctrine, theory, or belief." Hence this word means, etymologically, "the belief in what is uncovered or revealed," and its current meaning is "the belief in prophecies especially about the end of the world." REVEAL and REVELATION are from Latin and have to do with "removing the veil" (*velum*). This is why some people call the last book of the Bible the Apocalypse and some call it the book of Revelation. EUCALYPTUS (a type of tree) means "well covered" (*eu-* = "well" in Greek). Perhaps it has lots of leaves.

There are lots of interesting English words that begin with *apo-*. APOSTLE is from Greek *apostolos,* "one who is sent off (on a mission)." APOSTASY, "the abandonment of one's religion or other commitment," is from *apo-* and the root *sta-* "to stand." One who practices apostasy is an APOSTATE. APOSTROPHE has two different meanings but the same etymology (*apo-* "away" and *strephein* "to turn"). One is the punctuation sign that shows possession, etc. The other is "a turning away to address a person or abstraction that is not present" (e.g., "Death, be not proud . . ." from John Donne). APOCRYPHAL means currently "of questionable authenticity"; etymologically it means "hidden away" (*apo-* "away" and *kryptein* "to hide"). APOGEE means "the point of an orbit that is farthest from the earth" (*apo-* "from" and *ge-* "earth"). Finally, APOTHEOSIS means "deification," i.e., elevation to divine status, and it comes from *apo-*, "change," *theos*, "god," and *-sis*, "act of." DEIFICATION is derived from Latin and comes from the base of *deus,* "god," *fic-* from *facere,* "to make," and *-tion*, which forms abstract nouns.

B is for Bibliolatry.

BIBLIOLATRY means "devotion or concern for books." *Biblio-* is from *biblion*, which means "book" in Greek, and *-latry* is also from Greek and means "worship," as in IDOLATRY, "the worship of idols." (Greek *biblion* is from *biblos*, "papyrus," a plant that was used by the Egyptians, Greeks, and Romans as writing material.) Bibliolatry in moderation would not be a bad idea for students. Just as there are idolaters, and there is the adjective idolatrous, so too we have BIBLIOLATER and BIBLIOLATROUS. BIBLIOLATRY is the worship of books and BIBLIOMANIA is madness for books. Finally, BIBLIOMANCY is "divination by opening a book," especially the Bible, at random, pointing at a passage, and interpreting it as a sign of the future. There is a story about the person who woke up in the middle of the night and couldn't get back to sleep; so he decided to practice bibliomancy. He opened his Bible at random, and the first verse he saw was "Judas went out and hanged himself." Not liking that, he closed his Bible, opened it again and read, "Go thou and do likewise." Not liking this either, he tried a third time and got "What thou doest, do quickly."

We have several other words that begin with *bibli-*, e.g., BIBLICIST, "one who interprets the Bible literally." BIBLIOGRAPHY means *inter alia* a list of books used by an author. A BIBLIOPHILE is "a lover of books," and a BIBLIOPOLE is "one who sells books" (cf. the last two syllables of "monopoly"). *Bibliotheca* means "library" in Greek and there are derivatives in French, Spanish, Italian, and German. Finally there is BIBLIOTHERAPY, in which books are used to help individuals with personal problems. Notice that -*o*- is used to join elements in a compound word derived from Greek (e.g., BIBLI-O-LATRY).

From now on we will be speaking frequently of derivatives. For instance the English word PATERNAL ("pertaining to a father") comes from, or is derived from, the Latin word *pater* meaning "father." Paternal is, therefore, a derivative of *pater*. DERIVATIVE means "flows from" because *de*- means "from" and *riv*- is from *rivus*, "a stream or river." In this book we are dealing with words that "flow from" Latin and Greek. You will find knowing the Latin and Greek prefixes, suffixes, and roots that you can learn from this book a great blessing, and not a curse at all. Although English is a Germanic language in origin, it is estimated that 60% of our words come from Latin and Greek. In the sciences the figure is approximately 90%. What's more, the percentage coming from Greek is increasing since scientists, especially those in medicine, turn to Greek when they need to coin new words.

C is for Catastrophe.

A CATASTROPHE is "a calamity, a disaster." The adjective CATA-STROPHIC means "pertaining to a catastrophe." Etymologically CA-TASTROPHE means a "down turn," one of the meanings of *cata-* being "down" and *strophe* meaning "a turn" (from the verb *strephein*, "to turn"; another meaning of *strophe* is a stanza or verse of poetry). Did Roman writers who knew Greek and knew the meaning of *strophe* coin the word *versus*, a "verse," by analogy? (The Latin word for "to turn" is *verto, vertere*.) It could be; there are plenty of other examples. The *AHD* says that VERSE in this sense is from "a turning of the plow,"

hence, "a furrow, a line." There is also the rare word BOUSTROPHE-
DON, which refers to an ancient way of writing in which the first line
goes from left to right, the second from right to left, and so on (i.e., as
the *bous* [ox] turns when plowing; cf. Greek *bous* and English BOSS
and BOSSY, probably from Latin *bos*, which means "cow"). There is
also BOVINE, pertaining to a cow or buffalo. BOSS meaning "manager"
is from Dutch.

CATACLYSM is from a verb that means "to wash down," and one
of its current meanings is "a devastating flood." CATALYSIS is from a
verb that means "to break down," although, as one wit put it, there is
literally nothing down about catalysis and nothing up about analysis;
they are just two kinds of *lysis*. There is also CATARACT, "a huge water-
fall" from *catarassein*, "to rush down." CATARACT meaning "opacity
of the lens of the eye," according to the *AHD*, is probably from "a
comparison to a portcullis or other falling impediment or covering."
(It would be a good idea to look PORTCULLIS up in a dictionary that
has pictures!)

There is also CATALOGUE, in which *cata-* means "thoroughly" and
-logue is from *legein*, "to gather."

Cata- can also lose its final *-a* if it is prefixed to a word that begins
with *h-* as in CATHEDRAL, CATHOLIC, and CATHARSIS. A CATHEDRA
is a bishop's official throne, coming from *cata-* and *hedra*. This throne
is located in a cathedral. *Hedra*, by the way, is cognate with the Latin
verb *sedeo, sedere*, which means "to sit." COGNATE comes from Latin
nascor, nasci, natus meaning "to be born." Cognate means etymologically "born together."

In CATALYSM, *cata-* merely intensifies the meaning of the base
word. The word CATHOLIC with a small *c* means "universal" and
comes from *cata-* and *holos*, which means "whole." *Holos* is also found
in HOLISTIC and HOLOCAUST (originally a sacrifice in which the vic-
tim was wholly consumed by flames). One meaning of CATHARSIS is
"a cleansing of the emotions," which, according to Aristotle, can be
the effect of experiencing a tragedy in the theater.

Ch is for Chiromancy.

CHIROMANCY is a fancy name for PALMISTRY (i.e., "the art of predicting people's futures by reading their palms"). One used to find people doing this at carnivals. *Chir-* is from Greek *cheir*, which means "hand." The second part of the word, *-mancy*, is from the Greek word *mantis*, "a prophet," and the related noun *manteia*, which means "divination" (i.e., "the art of predicting the future"). *Chir-* is also found in CHIROPRACTOR, "one who practices CHIROPRACTIC," the medical practice of curing people's ills by manipulating the spine or other bones and bodily parts. Chiropractors are not MDs, but many people have great faith in them anyway. A CHIROPODIST, on the other hand, is an MD who treats hands and feet (*pod-* is from the Greek word for "foot"; compare Latin *ped-*, English "foot"/"feet," and German *Fuss*, all of which come from PIE **ped-/*pod-*). Note that PIE *p* survives in Latin and Greek but becomes *f* in English and German, and PIE *d* survives in Latin and Greek but becomes *t* in English and *ss* in German. We will see more examples of these correspondences.

CHIROGRAPHY is a word you won't see often, but if you encounter it, you should be able to guess its meaning—"handwriting" (also called "penmanship"). CHIRON (Greek *Cheiron*) was a wise and immortal centaur who tutored many Greek heroes, such as Jason and Achilles. Some sources say *Cheiron* is derived from the word for "hand." Centaurs, by the way, were human from the waist up but had the body of a horse. They were common in Greek mythology. CENTAUR is from *kentauros,* etymology unknown, something that is true for many words.

A veritable monster that also begins with *ch-* is the Chimera. Its front resembled a lion; its rear resembled a snake, and it was a she-goat in the middle with a second head rising from the creature's back. In addition it breathed fire. The hero Bellerophon killed the Chimera by hurling his spear at it as he rode over it with the help of Pegasus, the winged horse. The tip of his spear was equipped with a lump of lead that was melted by the Chimera's fiery breath. Today CHIMERA means "a fanciful mental illusion or fabrication" (*AHD*).

D is for Dyslexia.

There is a Latin saying: *Repetitio est mater studiorum,* which can be translated thus: "Repetition is the mother of studies." More freely one might say "The best way to learn anything is to repeat it over and over." Naturally this is controversial, but we are testing the truth of the saying by reiterating the prefix *dys-. Dys-* basically means "bad." (Compare it with the prefix *mal-,* which is from Latin.) DYSLEXIA is a reading disorder suffered by people with normal intelligence. The related adjective is DYSLECTIC. Both words come from *dys-* and *legein,* "to gather" hence "to read." DYSPEPSIA is "bad digestion" (*pepsia* = "digestion"). I wonder if the makers of Pepsi thought or hoped it would aid digestion? There is lots of debate online about this, but I am not taking sides. DYSPHAGIA is "difficulty in swallowing." PHAGOCYTES are "cells that 'eat' waste material in the blood." (*Phago-* is from the Greek verb *phagein,* which means "to eat," and *-cyte* is from Greek *cute, cyte,* which means "cell.") DYSPNEA is "difficulty in breathing." DYSTROPHY is a word from Greek that is perfectly parallel to MAL-NUTRITION, which is from Latin. Both words mean "bad nutrition." Muscular DYSTROPHY is widely known. (By the way, MUSCLE is from Latin *musculus,* which means "little mouse." Make a fist, bend your arm, and show off your *musculus.*)

A EULOGY is "a speech that praises someone." What would you call a speech that attacks someone? A DIATRIBE, but you might expect the opposite of eulogy to be DYSLOGY (coined by me, your author). UTOPIA and UTOPIAN are common English words. Now you can guess what the opposites would be, namely DYSTOPIA and DYSTOPIAN. A DYSTOPIA would be an imaginary "bad place." (I must point out immediately, however, that UTOPIA does not come from *eu* and *topia* but from *ou* and *topia,* which means "no place.") Two more learning disabilities are DYSGRAPHIA and DYSPHASIA. The first deals with writing and the second with speaking. Finally we conclude with two hybrid words: DYSFUNCTION and DYSCALCU-LIA ("difficulty with math"). In both of these words the Greek prefix *dys-* has been added to Latin bases. I don't like hybrid words, but it is futile to wage war against them. There will be more and more of them as time marches on.

Please don't diss these *dys-* words. They may come in handy someday!

E is for Eupeptic.

EUPEPTIC means "pertaining to *eupepsia*," which is "good digestion" in Greek. It is the opposite of DYSPEPTIC, "pertaining to bad digestion," something to be avoided if possible. *Eu-* is a prefix that means "good" or "well." It is found in such words as EUPHEMISM, EUPHONY, EUPHORIA, and EULOGY. *Dys-* is a prefix that means the opposite, as discussed in "D is for Dyslexia." EUPHEMISM is from *eu-* and *pheme* ("speech") and is "a kind way of saying something," while DYSPHEMISM would be a crude or cruel way of asserting something (e.g., using a derogatory, offensive, or vulgar term, and calling someone a pig or a chicken or a dog). Examples of euphemisms are "passed away" instead of "died" or "put to sleep" instead of "EUTHANIZED," which is from *eu-* and *thanatos*, Greek for "death." EUPHONY means "sounding well or agreeably." A symphony orchestra should sound euphonic since all the musicians are playing together (*sym-*), or should be. DYSPHONIA is "difficulty in speaking." EUPHORIA is defined as "a feeling of well-being"; DYSPHORIA is "a state of anxiety or discomfort." (By the way the Latin prefix *dis-* as in DISAPPEARANCE, is not related to Greek *dys-*.)

Finally a EULOGY, as mentioned above, is "a speech in praise of someone" (e.g., at a funeral). DYSLOGY doesn't exist in English (it could and it would be the opposite of a eulogy, i.e., an attack on someone) but DYSLEXIA does, and it was discussed in "D is for Dyslexia." The *-lexia* part of the word is related to the root *log-* (*lexia* = **leg-sia*) and has the *e*-grade of the root while *log-* has the *o*-grade. PIE roots typically have three forms, which are known as the "*e*-grade," the "*o*-grade," and the "zero-grade." This phenomenon is known as "ablaut." These vowel grades, or differences in vowel sounds, appear in words that are related to each other. Examples in English include the verb "sing, sang, sung" and the noun "song."

You won't see the word EUPNEA very often, but if you do, you should guess that it means "breathing normally." You may never see the word EUTROPHY, but you will see and hear DYSTROPHY as in "muscular dystrophy," which is characterized by the wasting away of muscles (as if from lack of nourishment).

Under "B is for Bibliolatry" it was pointed out that many English words are derived from Latin and Greek. Such words are called "derivatives" (e.g., PATERNAL from Latin *pater*, "father," and MATERNAL from Latin *mater*, "mother"). There is, however, another kind of relationship, which I am now introducing. If you look carefully at the English "father," Latin *pater*, Greek *patér*, and German *Vater*, you will notice some striking similarities, yet these words are not derived from each other. They are cognates, a concept that was explained above under "C is for Catastrophe." These modern words for "father" come from **pəter*, a word that must have existed in PIE. There is a simplified chart of the main branches of the Indo-European family of languages on page xii. A good place to learn about Proto-Indo-European is in the article "Indo-European and the Indo-Europeans" by Calvert Watkins, which can be found at the back of the *AHD*. By the way, the first vowel in **pəter* is called a schwa and was pronounced something like "uh." The asterisk that precedes *pəter* indicates that this is a hypothetical word that has not been found in any existing language. (Incidentally, ASTERISK means "little star." *Aster* is Greek for "star" [cf. ASTROLOGY] and *-isk* forms diminutives.)

G is for Gastronomic.

M. REEDY

GASTRONOMIC means "pertaining to GASTRONOMY," which is "the art or science of cooking." *Gastro-* is from the Greek word for "stomach," and *-nom-* is from the Greek *nomos,* "law," then "body of knowledge about a specific field" e.g., ECONOMY from Greek *oikos,* "house" (in which Greek *oik-* is Latinized to *oec-* and then simplified to *ec-*), and ASTRONOMY is "the study of the stars" (Greek *astron*). There is also the word GASTRONOMICAL, in which *-al* means "pertaining to," as does *-ic-*, which is why *-al* is optional. Other words from *gastro-* are GASTROENTEROLOGY, "the branch of medicine that deals with the stomach and the intestines" (*entera* in Greek, the "insides" hence the INTESTINES, which is from a Latin adverb *intus* that means "within"). There are also GASTROPODS ("mollusks such as the snail and the slug") that have a "stomach foot" for locomotion. *Pod-* is from Greek *pous, podos,* which means "foot" as was mentioned before. PODIUM is from *pod-*, as is ANTIPODES meaning "people whose feet are opposite ours" (i.e., they live opposite us on the globe and walk upside down from our perspective). There is also in medicine GASTRIC, GASTRITIS, GASTROLOGY, and GASTROSCOPE. Finally, a GASTRONOME or GASTRONOMIST (from Greek via French) is a "connoisseur of good food." French *connoisseur* is from Latin *cognosco, cognoscere*, which means "to know" and comes ultimately from PIE **gno-*, which also gives us our word "know."

H is for Hypercholesterolemia.

HYPERCHOLESTEROLEMIA indicates "an excessive amount of cholesterol in the blood." *Hyper-*, which is cognate with Latin *super-*, means "above," "beyond," and "exceedingly." CHOLESTEROL is from *chole*, Greek for "bile"; *ster-*, from *stereos*, means "solid" and *-ol* is a chemical suffix indicating a type of alcohol. The suffix *-emia* comes via Latin from Greek *haima*, "blood," which has the initial *h-* when it begins a word such as HEMATOLOGY ("the study of blood"), but lacks it when it is not initial (e.g., ANEMIA, which is etymologically "lack of blood," *an-* meaning "without"). By the way, Greek *haima* is Latinized to *haema* and the diphthong *ae-* is simplified to *e-*. To digress for a moment, I may have neglected to point out before that DIPHTHONG is a Greek word from *di-*, which means "two," and *phthongos*, "sound." (Yes, Greek had words that began with *phth-* and also *chth-* as in CHTHONIC, meaning "having to do with the underworld" from *chthon*, "earth." In a word such as CHTHONIC we speakers of English do not pronounce the initial *ch-* but the Greeks did. How do we know? Because we have inscriptions and manuscripts, and we can see that the ancient Greeks spelled words the way they pronounced them, something we don't always do.)

The opposite of *hyper-* is *hypo-*. *Hypo-* means "below," "under" as in HYPODERMIC (*derma* means "skin"). If *hypo-* comes before a Greek word beginning with *h*, it loses its *o* as in HYPHEN from *hypo-* and *hen* ("one"). Hyphen means etymologically "under one" (i.e., it causes two items to become one).

I is for Idea.

IDEA comes from Greek and is derived from a PIE root *weid-, *woid-, *wid-. These forms are the e-grade, the o-grade, and the zero-grade forms of the root. The zero-grade gives us in Latin *video*, which means "I see." With two suffixes in Greek it gives us *wid-es-ya, from which the word IDEA evolved. (The *w*, the *s*, and the *y* were eventually not pronounced.) IDEA for the Greeks, therefore, must have been the "look" of a thing, the mental picture. For example, the idea of a tree was originally the mental picture of the typical tree. Plato's "world of ideas" is also known as the "world of forms."

IDEAL means etymologically "pertaining to an idea." We also have IDEALIST, IDEALISM, and IDEALISTIC. There is also the verb IDEALIZE (i.e., "to make something ideal"). Coming through French we have *idée fixe*, which is "an obsession," definitely not a good thing. There is also IDEOLOGUE, "a person who is a promoter of an IDEOLOGY" ("the body of ideas and beliefs of a particular group"). Also from this root there is *Veda* and *Rig-Veda*, ancient Indian religious texts written in Sanskrit. *Veda* means "knowledge" illustrating the idea that what has been seen is known, and *Rig* means "sacred text."

A little over two hundred years ago there was a British judge named Sir William Jones, who was located in India. Perhaps because he had some spare time, he decided to study Sanskrit, the classical language of India. No doubt because he was well educated in Latin and Greek, he was astounded immediately by the similarities (e.g., the Sanskrit word for "father" is *pitar* and the word for "mother" is *matar*; compare Latin *pater* and *mater* and Greek *patēr* and *mētēr*). Influenced by Jones's discovery, scholars, especially in Germany, began identifying other languages that were related to English, Latin, Greek, and Sanskrit and belonged to what came to be called the Indo-European family of languages. There is a simplified chart of the main branches of the Indo-European family of languages on page xii. At the same time they began reconstructing PIE. The *AHD* contains an "Appendix of Indo-European Roots." Students are advised to consult this important resource. (The latest edition of the *AHD* also has an appendix of Semitic roots and an article on Proto-Semitic for those who know or are studying such languages as Hebrew and Arabic.)

Remember that words from different languages that descend from the same ancestral language, such as Greek *patér*, Latin *pater*, and English "father," are called cognates. The term "cognate" was defined above under "C is for Catastrophe." Consult that definition for review if necessary.

K is for Kaleidoscope.

Kal- is from the Greek *kalos*, which means "beautiful." It also appears as *kall-* (with two *l*'s) as in CALLIGRAPHY, which is "beautiful writing." (One who does it is a CALLIGRAPHER.) Remember that the Greek letter *kappa* shows up in English words sometimes as *k*, as in kudos, and sometimes as *c* as in CALISTHENICS, where *-sthen-* means "strength" and *-ic* means "pertaining to." The *eid-* in KALEIDOSCOPE is from the Greek word *eidos*, which means "form." *Eidos* originally began with *w-* and is related to Latin *video*, "I see." One might say that *eidos* is the "look" of a thing. A SCOPE is "a device for looking at something." Compare TELESCOPE, "a device for seeing far away," which is what *tele-* means. A PERISCOPE is "a device for looking around" (*peri-*), found mostly in submarines. A MICROSCOPE is "a device for looking at very small things" (*micro-*). SCOPE has the *o*-grade of this word. The *e*-grade is found in SKEPTICISM. A SKEPTIC is "a person who takes a 'hard look' at everything" and thus always appears to be doubtful.

The root *skep-* is interesting also because it appears as *spek-* (i.e., with the *p* and the *k* reversed). From *spek-* we have Latin-derived words such as SPECTACLE, SPECTRUM, SPECULATE, INSPECT, SUSPECT, INTROSPECT, RETROSPECT, and SPECIES. Actually, according to the *AHD* this form of the root (**spek-*) is the older form, **skep-* being an example of metathesis, a technical term in linguistics that means "the transposition of two sounds within a word." Saying "aks" instead of "ask" is an example of metathesis. (*Meta-* means "change," and *thesis* is "the act of putting or placing.") SKEPTIC is a word derived from Greek that has the **skep-* form of the root.

L is for Logos.

Logos means "word," "speech," and "reason." Some early Greek philosophers believed that *logos* in the sense of reason pervaded the universe making it intelligible to human reason. In Hellenistic Judaism *logos* is the word for "God." In Christianity the *Logos* is "the creative word of God" and is personified in Jesus. In English today *logos* is found in numerous words ending in *-logy*, "the study of," for instance THEOLOGY (*theos* means "god"), GEOLOGY (*ge* means "earth"), ANTHROPOLOGY (*anthropos* means "a human being"), COSMOLOGY (*cosmos* means "world"), PSYCHOLOGY (*psyche* means "soul"), etc.

Logos is also found as a suffix *-logue* meaning "speech" or "dialogue about," e.g., DIALOGUE (*dia-* often means "through," but sometimes, as here, can mean "between," so a dialogue is speech that occurs "between two or more people"). In EPILOGUE, however, *epi-*, which often means "on" and "around," means "after." In PROLOGUE, *pro-* means "before." In ANALOGUE, *ana-* (which can mean "up," "back," and "again") means "according to" and *logos* means "proportion." ECLOGUES are "pastoral poems." The word is parallel with "selections," which is from Latin and may have been the original meaning of "eclogue."

LOGIC is "the science of reasoning," and a LOGICIAN is an expert in it. A LOGOMACHY is "a battle of words," and LOGORRHEA could be defined as "a flood of words."

Ancient Greek philosophers defined a human being as a *zoon logikon* (i.e., "an animal endowed with reason and speech," which in Latin is *animal rationale*). This definitely does not mean that humans always act rationally!

M is for Metamorphosis.

METAMORPHOSIS means "a change in form or appearance" and is derived from Greek *meta-*, which can mean "after," "following," and often connotes "change" or "transformation." The suffix *-osis* means "condition," "action," or "process." TRANSFORMATION, which is from Latin, is of interest since it is parallel with METAMORPHOSIS, *meta-* and *trans-* meaning the same thing, as do *-osis* and *-tion*. Even more interesting is that the Latin word *forma* is perhaps borrowed (via Etruscan) from Greek *morphe* with transposition of the *m* and *f* sounds. (The Etruscans were a pre-Roman people whose civilization in Roman times was centered north of Rome in an area that is today called Etruria. There is evidence, however, that indicates they may have at one time occupied the whole Italian peninsula. The Etruscan language is not related to any known ancient language although it was written in an alphabet borrowed from the Greeks.)

METAPHYSICS, the most abstract field in philosophy, oddly enough has a very mundane etymology. We are told that the followers of Aristotle in the Middle Ages when they organized his works placed the most abstract works after the *Physics* and called them simply *meta ta physica*, which meant "after the *Physics*." Other sources say that the title *Metaphysics* may have been assigned as early as the first century BCE by one Andronicus of Rhodes. Since Latin doesn't have a definite article, the phrase *meta ta physica* became *meta physica,* and then one word.

Since the final *a* of *meta-* may be lost before another vowel in words beginning with a vowel or *h*, one must look carefully for this prefix. Consider for example METHOD, which is from *meta-* and *hodos* meaning "road" or "journey." (The ODOMETER, which shows how many miles you've traveled in your car, is also from *hodos*, "road," and "meter." Odometer comes to us from Greek *hodometer* via French. In the case of words borrowed from Greek, the French neither spelled nor pronounced initial *h*. Hence the loss of *h* in odometer.) METONY-MY is a figure of speech in which one word is used in place of another, with which it is associated. *Meta* normally loses its final *-a* when it is prefixed to a word beginning with a vowel, as before *onoma/onyma*, which means "name" in Greek. Metonymy is thus etymologically a change in name. For example, consider "The pen is mightier than the sword" meaning most likely "Journalism or literature is more powerful than armies." *Meta* normally loses its final -*a* when it is prefixed to a word beginning with a vowel, as before *onoma/onyma*, which means "name" in Greek. Metonymy is thus literally a change in name.

N is for Necrology.

Since *necro-* means "corpse" and then "death" and *-logy* usually means "the study of," one might guess that NECROLOGY means the "study of death," but that would be wrong. In this word, *-logy* is used in a more basic sense of "writing." Hence a NECROLOGY is "a list of people who have died." It is very much like an OBITUARY (from Latin *obire*, "to go to meet death"). NECROSIS is from *necro-* and *-sis* meaning "condition" and refers to the death of cells in living tissues. NECROPOLIS is etymologically "a city of the dead," hence a CEMETERY, which comes from the Latin *coemeterium*, from Greek *koimeterion* "a place for sleeping." NECROPHOBIA is "the fear of death or corpses," which is not really that unusual! NECROMANCY, the last part of which comes from *mantis*, a Greek word that means "prophet," is "contacting the dead (supposedly) to learn what the future holds." Finally NECROLATRY means "the worship of the dead" (cf. IDOLATRY).

While dealing with this subject I might point out another word the Greeks had for death, viz. *thanatos*. In Greek mythology Thanatos was the son of Night and Darkness and had a twin brother named Hypnos ("Sleep"). *Thanatos* seems to be more abstract than *necros*. "Thanatopsis" is a famous poem by William Cullen Bryant. The suffix *-opsis* means "glimpse of," but "Thanatopsis" has been translated as "A Meditation on Death." *Thanatos* was used by Freud for his hypothesized "death wish," which coexisted with an impulse for life. Sorry to be so LUGUBRIOUS (from Latin *lugubris*, "mournful," which is from *lugere* "to mourn").

Enough of this lugubrious talk. It's time to shout "*Viva, viva, viva!*" as the Italians and the Spanish do, meaning "Long life!"

O is for Orthodontia.

ORTHODONTIA (also known as ORTHODONTICS) is from *ortho-*, which means "straight" or "correct" in Greek, and *odont-*, the base of *odous*, the Greek word for "tooth." ORTHODONTIA is that part of dentistry that has to do with straightening teeth. A dentist who specializes in this field is naturally called an ORTHODONTIST. *Odont-* is, by the way, cognate with Latin *dens, dentis*, of which the base is *dent-*. Believe it or not, according to the *AHD*, *dens, dentis* is the present participle of the verb *edere*, which means "to bite" and then "to eat." (See **dent-* in Appendix I of the *AHD*.) (Participles are verbal adjectives, i.e., an adjective made from a verb, e.g., "the running dog." You might say that participles "participate" in the nature of both a verb and an adjective. The future passive participle always has *-nd-* in it, and it indicates something that is to be done, i.e., should be done. With some form of the verb "to be" it forms the "passive periphrastic" construction, truly a horrendous mouthful, but a few examples will clarify everything. The most famous example of this construction is *Carthago delenda est.* It is said that during the wars against Carthage the Roman Cato the Elder ended every speech before the Senate with *Carthago delenda est,* "Carthage must be destroyed.") Among the more interesting words with this root in it is DANDELION, which was originally spelled *dent-de-lion* and came from the French, who thought the leaves of the flower resembled the teeth of a lion.

But let us return to *ortho-*, which also appears in the adjective ORTHODOX and the noun ORTHODOXY. The *dox-* part of these words comes from Greek and means "an opinion," "a judgment," and "one's reputation," hence "honor, glory." Thus ORTHODOX means "having the straight (i.e., correct) opinion or belief." It is used primarily in religious contexts. *Doxa* meaning "glory" shows up in DOXOLOGY, "a hymn, usually short, of praise to God."

ORTHOGRAPHY has to do with correct (i.e., straight) spelling. ORTHOPEDICS is "the medical field that deals with deformities of the skeletal system," perhaps originally with deformities found in children, since the *ped-* part of the word comes from Greek *pais, paid-* meaning "child." This word was Latinized to *paes, paed-* and then simplified to *ped.* It should not be confused with the Latin word *pes, pedis*, which means "foot."

There is an order of insects called ORTHOPTERA, which includes locusts, crickets, and grasshoppers. Based on the name of the order, one would expect them to have straight wings since *ptera* means "wings" in Greek.

The opposite of ORTHODOX is HETERODOX, which comes from *hetero-* meaning "other." If your beliefs are heterodox they are "other than the correct ones." There was a time when people were burned at the stake for being heterodox!

P is for Paraphernalia.

PARAPHERNALIA originally meant "the property brought to a marriage by the bride other than her dowry" (*pherne* is the Greek word for "dowry"; it is from **pher-* "to carry"). Today this word means "personal property," and "stuff used in a special activity." The prefix *para-* means "beside," "alongside" (as in PARALLEL), "beyond" (as in PARANORMAL), "abnormal" (as in PARANOIA), and "assistant" (as in PARAMEDIC). A PARASITE in ancient Greece was "a person who got his food (*sitos*) from someone else." A PARADOX is "an abnormal belief (*doxa*)," and to PARAPHRASE is "to restate something in different words." The PARACLETE is the "Holy Spirit," the third person of the Trinity, the one called (Greek *kle-*) to one's side to help. A PARABLE is a "comparison" from *para-* and *ballein*, "to throw or place."

A PARENTHESIS is "a word, phrase, or sentence put or placed (Greek *the-*) in (*en*) a written passage, usually to explain." Notice that in PARENTHESIS *para-* loses its final *a* before a vowel. The suffix *-sis* means "condition," "process," or "action."

PARABLE means etymologically a "comparison." It comes from *parabale*, which means "to throw, to place beside." PARALYSIS and PARALYTIC, the latter of which means "relating to paralysis," are derived from a Greek verb, *paralyein*, which means "to disable." A PARODY is from *para* ("beside," "parallel," hence "mock") and *oide*, "a song."

The Greek word *para-* should not be confused with the Latin verb *paro, parare*, which means "to prepare." The Latin word gives us PARASOL, which prepares you for the sun (Latin *sol*), and PARACHUTE, which prepares you for the "chute," from Latin *cado, cadere*, "to fall." PARAPET, "a low wall," is from Latin *paro* and *pectus*, "chest," via Italian *petto*. Were parapets originally chest high? Most likely.

Ph is for Philanthropy.

PHILANTHROPY is quite simply "the love of one's fellow human beings." *Phil-* is from the Greek word for "love," and *-anthropy* is from the Greek word *anthropos*, which means "human being." We have many words in English that begin with *phil-* (e.g., PHILADELPHIA, "the city of brotherly love"; *adelphos* is Greek for "brother"). There is also PHILOSOPHY, "the love of wisdom" (Know any girls named Sophia? Is she unusually wise? Know any guys named Philip? If so, does he love horses? *-ip* is from *hippos*, "horse"). I am a PHILOLOGIST, and my specialty is PHILOLOGY, which is etymologically "the love of words." The opposite of PHILANTHROPY is MISANTHROPY, "the hatred of humankind." One who does it is a MISANTHROPE or MISANTHROPIST. There is a play by the French playwright Molière (1622–1673) named *The Misanthrope*. By the way, the last part of PLAYWRIGHT has nothing to do with writing, as one might think. It comes from an Anglo-Saxon root that means "work" and gives us WORK, and WROUGHT. An ERG is "a unit of work." It and ORGAN lost the initial *w*. Who would believe it? If you don't believe me, see **werg-* in Appendix I of the *AHD*.

From the Greek word for "human being," *anthropos*, we get ANTHROPOCENTRISM, "the belief that humans are the most important creatures in the universe," ANTHROPOLOGY, which is the study of human cultures and which many students take in college, ANTHROPOMORPHIC, which means literally "shaped like a human being," and finally, something I hesitate to mention, ANTHROPOPHAGY, "the practice of eating humans" also known as CANNIBALISM, which is from the allegedly cannibalistic Caribs of Cuba and Haiti (*AHD*). The root *phag-* meaning "eat" we find in PHAGOCYTES, "cells that eat waste material in the blood," as was mentioned under "D is for Dyslexia." Finally the ESOPHAGUS, which is from *oiso-* (simplified to *eso-*) "to carry" and *phagus*, carries what you eat to the stomach.

Ps is for Psychiatrist.

One might conclude from the number of words we have that begin with *psych-* that Americans are extremely interested in their
PSYCHES (i.e., their souls). We have "physicians of the soul" (PSY-
CHIATRISTS) and "therapy for the soul" (PSYCHOTHERAPY), which
often involves "analysis of the soul" (PSYCHOANALYSIS). We even try
to measure souls (PSYCHOMETRICS), write histories of them (PSY-
CHOHISTORY), drug them (PSYCHOPHARMACOLOGY), operate on
them (PSYCHOSURGERY), and listen to them (PSYCHOACOUSTICS).
(Actually the last field is the study of the perception of sounds,
which shows that etymology is not an infallible guide to the current
meaning of a word.) All this constitutes quite a PSYCHODRAMA, but
it doesn't exhaust the list of English words that begin with *psych-*.

Another Greek word that is popular among Americans is *pseudo-*,
which means "false." There is PSEUDONYM, which is a "pen name."
Onoma/onyma means "name" in Greek. Hence we have ANONYMOUS,
"without a name" (*a-, an-* = "not" and "without"), HOMONYM, "having the same sound" (*homo-* = "same"), and METONYMY, "a figure
of speech." *Met-* from *meta-* often connotes change, as mentioned
under "K is for Kaleidoscope." The use of "sword" for "armed forces"
is an example of METONYMY, which was explained above under "M
is for Metamorphosis." There is SYNONYM (*syn-* "with" here means
"same") and PSEUDONYM (already mentioned), "a false name" or "pen
name." In ONOMATOPOEIA the *-poeia* means "making" and here it is
of words that imitate what they refer to (e.g., "sis-boom-bah," "oink,"
and "meow").

Another word that begins with *ps-* is PSALM. (There's a whole
book of them in the Bible, as you probably know.) "One who com-
poses psalms" is a PSALMIST, and "a book of psalms" is a PSALTER. (I
wonder what happened to the *m*; most likely **psalmter* would give us
an impossible consonant cluster.)

I will end the discussion of *ps-* words with three rare ones. PSIT-
TACOSIS is "a disease of parrots that can spread to humans." (*Psittakos*
is the Greek word for parrot.) PSEPHOLOGY is "the study of elections,"

and it comes from *psephos,* "pebble," which is what the ancient Greeks used when voting. Finally PSORIASIS, a skin disease, is from *psora,* the Greek word for "itch."

It should be noted that, although we do not pronounce the initial *p-* in these words, it can be pronounced, and the ancient Greeks pronounced it. In this respect, I would say, they were more sensible than we are when it comes to orthography. (Remember that word?)

R is for Rheostat.

A RHEOSTAT is "a device that regulates the flow of electricity." The first part of the word comes from the Greek verb that means "to flow." We have the same verb in RHEOMETER, which is "a device for measuring the flow of liquids such as blood." RHEUM, by the way, is "a watery discharge from the eyes or nose" that was once thought to cause RHEUMATISM! There is also a word RHEUMATOID, in which the suffix -*oid* means "resembling, related to."

The early Greek philosopher Heraclitus, nicknamed "the Obscure" (*floruit* ca. 500 BCE), is famous for having said, "Everything is in a state of flux" (*Panta rhei* in Greek), and of course he was right. "You cannot step twice in the same river for other waters are ever flowing on" is another way he put it. He apparently meant that reality, although it is changing, is not chaotic because *Logos* ("the Word," also "Reason") pervades everything, including our minds. We should, therefore, try to make our reason conform to the universal Reason and live reasonably. In mythology, Rhea was a Titaness and the wife of the Titan Cronos and bore him six offspring, all gods, including Zeus, Hera, and Hades. The Titans, as you can see, ruled the universe before the gods according to Greek mythology. Our word TITANIC derives from the "monstrous power and size of the creatures preceding the rule of Zeus" (*Oxford Classical Dictionary*, s.v. "Titan").

The -*stat* part of RHEOSTAT comes from a Greek verb that means "to stand" and also "to cause to stand." Hence THERMOSTAT is "a device to regulate heat." STASIS means "standing still" and in medicine it can refer to "blood that is not flowing through an artery or vein," which even a person not trained in medicine knows is a serious problem!

If you experience ECSTASY and become ECSTATIC, you are "standing outside (*ek-*) yourself." On the other hand, if you APOSTATIZE and become an APOSTATE, you have "taken a stand away from (*apo-*) your religion." A STABLE (noun) is "a standing place for horses and cattle." STABLE (adjective) means "not moving or changing." An OBSTACLE is "a little something that is standing in your way." SUBSTANCE is from the Latin *sub-* and *stare* and means "to stand under, to be present." Finally the summer SOLSTICE occurs around June 21, and the winter SOLSTICE occurs around December 21 (in the northern hemisphere). On these days the sun (*sol* in Latin) appears to stand still. STABLE, OBSTACLE, SUBSTANCE, and SOLSTICE are derivatives that show that the root *sta-* is found in both Greek and Latin with the same meaning. In SOLSTICE the root *sta-* has been weakened to *sti-*.

S is for Sophistry.

The Sophists, with whom Socrates liked to argue, were described by one of my teachers as "itinerant university professors without a university base." In other words they were wandering scholars who moved from city-state to city-state in fifth-century BCE Greece before there were any institutions of higher learning. A number of Plato's dialogues depict Socrates showing that the Sophists didn't know what they were talking about (i.e., they hadn't thought deeply about their subjects). Today SOPHIST has a complimentary meaning ("a scholar or thinker") and a derogatory one ("one skilled in elaborate and devious argumentation"). One meaning of SOPHISTIC is "relating to the Sophists." SOPHISTRY means "plausible but fallacious argumentation." (FALLACIOUS, which is from Latin, means "full of FALLACIES," which are "false statements.") SOPHOMORE is derived from Greek *sophos*, "wise," and *moros*, "stupid." I leave it to readers to guess what this says about those in the second year of high school or college. Above we mentioned girls named Sophia. You could expect them to be wise. Sophocles (490–406 BCE) was one of the greatest of all authors of tragedies. His name means etymologically "famous for wisdom" (-*cles* = "famous for").

Let me discuss some more Latin words in anticipation of the second section of this book. MORON ("stupid" or "foolish"), MORONIC, MORONITY, and MORONISM, from the Greek *moros*, were once in common use, but are now considered offensive. While we are on this subject, we might as well look at STUPID, STUPIDITY, and STUPOR, which are from Latin *stupere*, "to be stunned." A synonym for stupid is OBTUSE. OBTUSE is from Latin *obtundere*, which means "to make dull by striking." The participle is *obtusus* and means "dull, blunted."

The verb RETARD means "to cause to move slowly." RETARDED means "slowed down," "developing later than normal." It is from the Latin verb *retardare* which means "to delay, to cause to move more slowly." It is now considered offensive when applied to people. Compare TARDY. There is also "behindhand" which you'll probably never hear or see although it is a wonderful word. "Beforehand" is much more common.

T is for Telepathy.

The word TELEPATHY, "the purported transmission of information from one person to another without using any of our known sensory channels," consists of two Greek elements: *tele-*, which means "distant" or "far away," and *path-*, "feeling," "perception." There was great interest in the subject in the nineteenth century, but few people believe in it today, and there is no scientific evidence that it actually occurs. Other words that begin with *tele-* are TELEPHONE (*phone* = Greek for "sound, voice"), TELEGRAPH, and TELEGRAM (-*graph* and -*gram* come from the Greek verb *graphein* "to write"). A TELESCOPE is "a device for looking at things that are far away," as was pointed out in "K is for Kaleidoscope." TELEVISE and TELEVISION derive from -*vise* and -*vision*, which come from Latin *visus*, the fourth principal part of the verb *video, videre*, "to see." (Principal parts will be explained in the Latin section.) Remember that words that consist of elements from different languages are called "hybrid" words. The word HYBRID itself is from Latin *hybrida/hibrida*, "an animal produced from two different species."

There are lots of other English words that begin with *t* and are derived from Greek. For example, TAUTOLOGY comes from Greek *to auto*, which means "the same" and -*logy*, here "to say." "Business is business" is an example of a tautology. It is TAUTOLOGOUS. Another interesting *t* word from Greek is TRAGEDY, which comes from *tragos*, "goat," and *oide*, "song." There have been many attempts to explain the etymology of TRAGEDY. The two most plausible are (1) that the members of the tragic chorus were dressed as satyrs, mythological half-humans that were goats from the waist down, or (2) that, since plays were performed in competitions, the prize for the best may have been a goat. Goats were sacred to the god Dionysus (the Romans called him Bacchus, as did the Greeks sometimes). Two final words from Greek that begin with *t* are TYRANNICIDE, "the murder of a tyrant" (cf. HOMICIDE), and TYRANNOSAURUS, "a large meat-eating dinosaur" from *tyrannos* (Greek for "tyrant") and *sauros* (Greek for "lizard"). The tyrannosaurus was one of the largest carnivorous dinosaurs that ever lived.

Th is for Theocracy.

THEOCRACY means "rule by god," and one who believes in it is a THEOCRAT, just as DEMOCRACY means "rule by the people," and one who believes in it is a DEMOCRAT. The last part of these words is from the Greek word *kratos*, which means "power" or "rule." *Theos* is the Greek word for "god," and it is found in THEISM and ATHEISM. The *a* in ATHEISM is called "alpha privative." It connotes absence or negation. Before a word beginning with a vowel it is spelled *an-*, as in ANARCHY, which means "without a ruler." THEODORE means "gift of god," as does DOROTHY. Another beautiful name is THEOPHILUS, which could mean "beloved of god" or "loving god." Finally there is THEODICY and THEOSOPHY. THEODICY is etymologically the "justification of god" or better "the rational justification for belief in god," which is also called "natural theology." For some, THEODICY is the justification for belief in god in spite of the evil in the world. THEOSOPHY, which is from *theos*, "god," and *sophia*, meaning "wisdom," is defined as "religious philosophy or speculation about the nature of the soul based on mystical insight into the nature of God" (*AHD*).

St. Gregory Thaumaturgus is also known as St. Gregory the Miracle-worker (213–270 CE). *Thaumat-* means "wonder" in Greek, and *-urgus* is from *ergon,* the Greek word for "work" (see above in "Ph is for Philanthropy"). The abstract word is THAUMATURGY, "the working of miracles." A THERMOMETER measures heat and a THERMOSTAT is "a device for regulating temperatures." THEATER, THEORY, and THEOREM are from Greek *thea*, "a viewing." The first is "a place for viewing things"; a theory and a theorem could be based on a vision.

There are many other interesting words that begin with *th-*. One of them is THESAURUS, which is the Greek word for the "treasury." Currently a thesaurus is "a reference work that lists words with their synonyms and antonyms." A thesaurus comes in very handy if you can't think of the exact word you want. *Roget's Thesaurus* is one of the most famous.

X is for Xerophthalmia.

XEROPHTHALMIA is a medical term that means "dryness of the eye." *Xero-* comes from the Greek word for "dry," and *ophthalmos* is the Greek word for "eye." The suffix *-ia* makes it an abstract noun. There are some other medical terms that begin with *xero-* (e.g., XEROSIS meaning "dryness"). It could be of the skin (XERODERMIA) or of the mouth (XEROSTOMIA). The branch of medicine that deals with eyes is called OPHTHALMOLOGY, and one who practices it is an OPHTHALMOLOGIST. Ophthalmologists use an OPHTHALMOSCOPE to examine eyes.

There are a few other English words that begin with *xero-* besides xerophthalmia (e.g., XEROPHILOUS, which refers to plants such as cacti that love hot, dry climates; remember that *phil-* has to do with "love"). Finally there is XEROX, a trademark. Secretaries and other office workers were extremely happy when Xerox machines came on the market in 1959. Previously to make copies they had to pour fluids into copy machines. Here was a copier that worked without water! The Xerox 914 came on the market in 1959 and is one of the most successful products of all time.

English does not have many words that begin with *x*-, nor does Greek have many words that begin with an *x* sound. The *AHD* has only two and one-half pages of *x*-words. There are a few words that begin with *xeno*-, which in Greek means "strange," "foreign," and "different," such as XENOLITH, "a rock fragment foreign to the igneous mass in which it occurs." There is also XENOPHOBIA, "the fear of strangers and of foreign things." Fortunately there is XENOPHILIA to counterbalance it, although the term is very rare. There is finally XYLOPHONE. Xylophones are usually made of wood, which is what *xylo*- means. A XYLOGRAPH is "an inscription on wood," and a XYLOPHAGE is "an organism that eats wood." How wonderful it is to know all these rare words! One of my goals is to make all my readers *amatores verborum rarorum*, "lovers of rare words!"

Z is for Zoophobia.

ZOOPHOBIA is "an abnormal fear of animals." *Zoon* is the Greek word for "animal," and we have many derivatives of it in English. Zoo, of course, is short for "zoological garden." ZOOLOGY is that part of biology that deals with animals. ZOOTOMY treats of the anatomy and dissection of animals. (Note that DISSECTION comes from Latin *dis-* "apart" and *sectare* "to cut"). ZOOMORPHISM is "the attribution of animal characteristics or qualities to a god." Remember that *morphe* is the Greek word for "form," and in fact, Latin *forma* "form" may come (via Etruscan) from *morphe* with the *m* and the *f* sounds transposed, as was discussed above under "M is for Metamorphosis." ZOOLATRY is "the worship of animals." In other words, some peoples have gods that resemble animals. ZOONOSIS refers to "the diseases of animals that can be transmitted to humans"; PSITTACOSIS (from parrots) has been mentioned above under "Ps is for Psychiatrist." Rabies is the best known example of zoonosis. *Zoo-* is not always the first syllable in the word. There is for instance PROTOZOA (plural noun) and PROTOZOAN (adjective). *Proto-* means "first, earliest." *Zoon* is a living being. The plural is *zoa*.

We began this page with ZOOPHOBIA. If you're curious about phobias, there is online "The Phobia List." There is simply no limit to the number of things people can fear! Here are ten examples (not necessarily the strangest): ANTHOPHOBIA, "fear of flowers," BUFONOPHOBIA, "fear of toads," CLINOPHOBIA, "fear of going to bed," EUPHOBIA, "fear of hearing good news," HEDONOPHOBIA, "fear of feeling pleasure," LOGIZOMECHANOPHOBIA, "fear of computers," MYXOPHOBIA, "fear of slime" (also called BLENNOPHOBIA), NEPHOPHOBIA, "fear of clouds," OCTOPHOBIA, "fear of the number eight," PHOBOPHOBIA, "fear of phobias." I would not bother to memorize any of these unless you just want to impress your friends.

Words Derived from Latin

A is for Antepenultimate.

Ante is a Latin preposition and prefix that means "before" and "in front of." Used as a noun it means in English "the money each poker player must put into the 'kitty' before receiving any cards." (Why those contributions are called "kitty" isn't known.) Don't confuse *ante* with *anti-*, the latter of which comes from Greek and means "against" as in ANTIFREEZE and ANTIDISESTABLISHMENTARIAN- ISM, which in the *Oxford English Dictionary* is defined as "opposition to the disestablishment of the Church of England (rare)," but popularly cited as an example of a long word. (It consists of twenty-eight letters.) But I digress.

The meanings of ANTEROOM and ANTEDATE are obvious. ANTE- BELLUM means "before the war," especially the American Civil War. ANTEDILUVIAN means "extremely old, before the flood" (especially the flood of Noah described in Genesis). In grammar, an ANTECED- ENT is a noun or phrase that "goes before" (*ante-* = "before" and *ced-* = "goes") a noun to which the pronoun refers.

Pen- is from Latin *paene*, which means "almost"; for instance a PENINSULA means etymologically "almost an island" (*insula*), and PENUMBRA means etymologically "almost a shadow" (*umbra*). UL- TIMATE is from Latin *ultimatus*, which is from the verb *ultimare* meaning "come to the end." ANTEPENULTIMATE, therefore, means "coming before the next to the last." For example, the antepenulti- mate syllable in "antidisestablishmentarianism" is *-ri-*.

Now look for an opportunity to impress your friends with one of these SESQUIPEDALIAN words! (*Sesquipedalis* in Latin means "a foot and one-half long." *Sesqui* = "one and one half" as in SESQUICENTENNI- AL, "a period of 150 years," and *ped-* is from the Latin word for "foot.")

B is for Benediction.

BENEDICTION etymologically means "speaking well of someone." The current meaning is "a blessing" or "a call for a blessing from God." Other words that begin with *bene-* are BENEFACTOR and BENEFACTRESS. The first is "a man who helps others, especially with financial aid," and the second is a woman who does the same. BENEFICIAL means "helpful" or "advantageous." A BENEFIT is something that "promotes well-being" and a BENEFICIARY is usually "one who receives money" (e.g., from an insurance policy). If you travel in Italy, you'll hear people saying *bene* and *molto bene* constantly, meaning "well," "right," and "very well." In France it's *bien* and *très bien*, and in Spain it's *bien* and *muy bien*. The ancient Romans most likely said *bene* and *multo bene*.

Words that begin with *male-* mean the opposite of words that begin with *bene-*. Hence MALEDICTION means "a curse" or "slander." A MALEFACTOR is an evildoer. The root *-fact-* is from the verb meaning "to make" or "to do," and the suffix *-or* indicates "a person who does something."

The second part of the word BENEDICTION comes from a Latin verb. Regular Latin transitive verbs have four principal parts. (English verbs tend to have only three principal parts, e.g., see, saw, seen.) The four parts of the Latin verb *dico*, meaning "to say" are *dico, dicere, dixi, dictus*. The *dict-* in BENEDICTION comes from the fourth principal part of *dico*, namely *dictus*. The suffix *-ion* indicates an "action," "state of being," or "the result of an action." BENEDICTION, therefore, means the "act of speaking well of someone or something" (i.e., blessing it).

Nota bene: In this book I give the first or second principal part of verbs (e.g., *dico* or *dicere*) and the base of the last principal part (e.g., *dict-*). A list of verbs with all four principal parts can be found in the appendix. (*Nota bene* means "note well." It is often abbreviated n.b.)

C is for Convalescence.

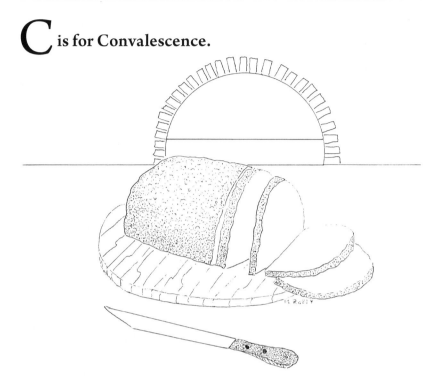

CONVALESCENCE is "the return to good health after an illness." The person who is becoming well is described as CONVALESCENT.

Cum is a Latin preposition that means "with," as when a student graduates *cum laude*, "with praise," or *magna cum laude*, "with great praise." (Note that with a phrase such as this, the Romans liked to put the adjective before the preposition, something we cannot do in English.) *Cum* as a prefix can take the form of *co-, col-, com-, con-,* or *cor-* depending on the following letter (e.g., COMPANION, CONSPIRATOR, COLLABORATOR, COOPERATE, and CORRESPONDENT). Sometimes this prefix does not have the meaning "with," but it simply intensifies the meaning of the base of the word.

A COMPANION, by the way, is "someone you break bread with" (*panis* is "bread" in Latin); CONSPIRATORS breathe together, COLLABORATORS work together, CORRESPONDENTS respond with one another, and to COOPERATE means "to work together." If you become an "etymological thinker" (i.e., one who thinks about the origin of words), words will often bring an image to mind (e.g., of conspirators hunched over around a table in the back room "breathing together" as they plot some nefarious action). (NEFARIOUS is from Latin *nefas,* "sinful," "unlawful," or "contrary to divine command." *Ne-* means "not" and *fas,* "that which is lawful," "right." Cf. FATE from *fatum,* "what has been spoken by the gods." *Fa-* is cognate with the Greek *phe-/pha-* "to speak," as in PROPHET. To say that *fa-* and *phe-/pha-* are cognates means that they are derived from the same PIE root.)

Back to CONVALESCENCE, *val-* is from *valere* "to be strong" and *valescere* means "to begin to be strong," *-esce-* being a suffix that forms "inceptive" verbs in Latin, e.g., CRESCENT, ADOLESCENT, RUBESCENT ("becoming red"), LAPIDESCENT ("becoming rock"), QUIESCENT, and RECRUDESCENT ("growing raw again"). All the verbs have the idea of becoming something.

The Romans used the verb *valere* to say "goodbye" (e.g., *vale* = "farewell" to one person, and *valete* to more than one). *Ave* and *avete* were used both to greet and bid farewell. Now you know what to say in case you encounter an ancient Roman somewhere.

D is for Decomposition.

De-, which usually means "down," "away," or "from," can also indicate (as here) "reversal," "undoing." *Com-* usually means "with," "together," and *posit-* is from the last principal part of the verb *pono*, which means "put" or "place." The suffix *-ion* forms abstract nouns and indicates an action or result of an action. COMPOSITION is, therefore, "the act of putting the parts together to form a whole" and DECOMPOSITION is taking it apart. A word deriving from Greek that is parallel to COMPOSITION is SYNTHESIS, where *syn-* means "together," *the-* is from a verb that means "put" or "place," and *-sis* means "state of" or "result of."

DISINTEGRATION is a word with a meaning similar to decomposition. The prefix *dis-* is from Latin and can mean "not" as in DISSIMILAR, "opposite of" as in DISFAVOR, and "undo," "do the opposite of," as in DISARRANGE and DISINTEGRATE ("to be reduced to parts"). INTEGRATE means "to make into a whole by bring all the parts together" and is from INTEGER meaning "whole," "intact," or "untouched" (from *in-*, "not," and *tag-*, *teg-* meaning "touch"). DISINTEGRATION, therefore, means something like "the state resulting from the undoing of the oneness of something."

Sorry to be so destructive under *d*. It has nothing to do with the fourth letter of the alphabet. I promise to be more constructive from now on.

E is for Egregious.

Ex- (also just *e-*) is a very common prefix that means "out of," "away from," and "former" as in EX-PRESIDENT. EXHALE is "to breathe out," INHALE is "to breathe in"—both from Latin *halo* "to breathe" (cf. HALI-TOSIS); EXHUME is "to remove from the ground," EXIT means literally "it goes out," and *Ex nihilo nihil fit* means "out of nothing nothing comes." (This is the obvious sort of thing philosophers like to assert.)

EGREGIOUS means etymologically "out of the flock" (*grex, gregis* means "flock" in Latin; the base is *greg-*). Currently EGREGIOUS means "very bad," "flagrant" (e.g., an "egregious blunder"). Suppose, for example, you are about to shake the president's hand, and you step on his or her toe. That would be an "egregious blunder." FLAGRANT, by the way, means "flaming" or "blazing" and is from a Latin verb that means "to burn, blaze." Latin *grex, gregis* also gives us GREGARIOUS, which refers to a person who loves the company of others (i.e., other members of the flock).

The Perth Academy, which is located in Perth, Scotland, has a wonderful motto on its coat of arms. It is *Pro Rege, Lege et Grege*, which means "For the King, the Law, and the Flock," that is "the People." Not only is it inclusive, it rhymes! (Incidentally, RHYMES and RIMES are apparently the same except for the fact that the spelling of "rhymes" was influenced by the spelling of the word "rhythm.")

F is for Frugivorous.

There is quite a list of words ending in *-vorous* (e.g., FRUGIVOROUS, HERBIVOROUS, CARNIVOROUS, GRAMINIVOROUS, OMNIVOROUS, and INSECTIVOROUS). For each of these adjectives there is a corresponding noun—FRUGIVORE, HERBIVORE, CARNIVORE, GRAMINIVORE, OMNIVORE, and INSECTIVORE. A FRUGIVORE eats fruits (Latin *frux, frug-*); an HERBIVORE eats plants (Latin *herba*); a CARNIVORE eats flesh (Latin *caro, carn-*); a GRAMINIVORE eats grass (Latin *gramen, gramin-*); an OMNIVORE will eat anything (Latin *omni-*, "all," "every"); and an INSECTIVORE eats insects. (INSECTIVORE comes from the Latin *insectum*, "cut in" in imitation of Greek *entomon*, also "cut in." *En* in Greek means "in" and the root *tom-* means "to cut." ATOM means "can't be cut or split"! Insects have segmented bodies, i.e., their bodies have "cuts" in them.) The word VORACIOUS ("desiring to eat large amounts of food") also comes from the Latin *vorare*, "to eat."

Latin has another word for "to eat," namely *edo* (root = **ed-*). It gives us EDIBLE meaning "suitable for eating." *Ed-* is cognate with our word eat which means, as was explained earlier in "C is for Catastrophe," that both words are derived from the same PIE root, which is **ed-*. Our word "dental" is from *dens, dentis*, the present participle of **ed-* in the sense of "biting." I hope this whets your appetite for more PIE roots.

Latin nouns come in groups called "declensions." Nouns such as *alumna* and *insecta* belong to the first declension. Nouns such as *alumnus* are in the second declension. In the third declension the base of a word often cannot be found in the first form so a second form must be given. *Frux, frugis* ("fruit"), *caro, carnis* ("flesh"), and *gramen, graminis* ("grass") are examples. By removing the *-is* of the second form, we get the base that shows up in English derivatives.

Prandium in Latin means "late breakfast" or "lunch." Believe it or not, the *-d-* in this word is probably related to *ed-* mention above. But enough of this—go now and take a postprandial circumambulation and digest what you can of this.

G is for Grandiloquence.

GRANDILOQUENCE is defined as speech that is "pompous or bombastic" (*AHD*). (POMPOUS, by the way, means "full of pomp," which comes from Latin *pompa* and ultimately from Greek *pompe*, "a procession" or "parade." BOMBASTIC means "pertaining to bombast," which comes via French, from medieval Latin *bombax* meaning "cotton." The French word meant "cotton padding." I leave it to readers to guess what cotton padding has to do with lofty speech.) Returning to GRAND, lots of things in English are grand. For example, dukes and duchesses and dames, rivers and canyons, mothers and fathers, nieces and nephews, slams, pianos, and tours, and also juries, operas, and marches. Finally let us not forget GRANDIOSE meaning "full of grandeur." (The suffixes *-ose* and *-ous* mean "full of." These suffixes will appear frequently from now on.)

The Latin verb *loquor, loqui, locutus* means "to talk" and gives us LOQUACIOUS, which is not a compliment; CIRCUMLOCUTION, "a roundabout way of saying something"; ELOQUENT, from "speaking out"; OBLOQUY (*ob-* can mean "against"), a synonym of CALUMNY, which means "slander"; SOLILOQUY (*sol-* is from *solus*, "alone"); and VENTRILOQUIST, "one who speaks from the stomach" (*venter, ventri-*) (i.e., one who is able to project the voice so it appears to be coming from elsewhere).

Under "F is for Frugivorous" I advised readers to take a "postprandial circumambulation," and above I used CIRCUMLOCUTION. I assume most readers know that *circum* means "around" because of common words such as CIRCUMFERENCE (of a circle), CIRCUMNAVIGATE (e.g., the world), and CIRCUMSCRIBE (literally "to write around"). AMBULATION is from Latin *ambulare* "to walk" as in "the patient was ambulatory." AMBULANCE is from the French *hôpital ambulant*, literally "walking hospital," that is, one that could be taken apart and moved with the army as it advanced or retreated. Only later did it come to refer to a vehicle for transporting patients to a hospital.

Back to GRANDILOQUENCE. When you finish this book, you could become a grandiloquent speaker, but I hope you don't!

H is for Homicide.

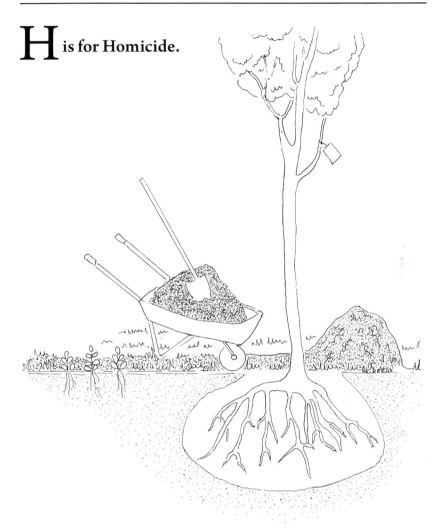

HOMICIDE is both an abstract noun ("he was guilty of homicide") and a concrete noun ("the police are searching for the homicide"). *Homo* is the Latin word for "human being" as in *Homo sapiens* (*sapiens* means "wise," "knowing" and comes from the verb *sapio, sapere* "to know"). *Homo* meaning "human being" should not be confused with the Greek adjective *homo-*, which is a totally different word meaning "same." If you look up *homo* in a Latin dictionary, you will find that it is given as *homo, hominis*; the second form is called the "genitive" and it indicates possession (*inter alia*). Knowing the genitive is important because many English derivatives come from the genitive, not the nominative. An example is *homin-*, which is found by removing the *-is* from the genitive. A word such as HOMINOID, which means "resembling a human being," consists of *homin-* and *-oid*, a Greek suffix that means "shaped like or resembling."

HOMICIDE means "the killing of a human being" (the suffix *-cide* is from the Latin verb *caedere* that means "to strike or kill"). Compare PESTICIDE and INSECTICIDE.

There is a Latin word *humus*, which means "soil, earth." It has come into English unchanged, and it refers to organic matter in the soil that comes from the decomposition of plants and animals. The point of this is that *homo* meaning "man" is related to *humus* meaning "soil," and this tells us that the Romans (and their ancestors) thought of humans as "earthlings." Also a HUMBLE person is close to the ground. To INHUME means "to bury" (i.e., place in the earth), and to EXHUME is to remove from the earth. All of this should be humbling for us humans.

I is for Ineffable.

In the word INEFFABLE, the *in-* means "not." The *ef-* is from *ex-*, "out," and the root *fa-* comes from Latin *for, fari, fatum*, which means "to speak." The suffix *-able* means "capable of" or "worthy of." Hence IN-EFFABLE means "incapable of being put into words" as in the phrase "the ineffable majesty of God." The root *fa-* is also found in FABLE ("a story"), FABULOUS ("full of fables"), INFANT ("unable to speak"), FANE, a rare word meaning "shrine" (i.e., "where one speaks to the gods"), and PROFANE and PROFANITY, "what is said outside a temple," hence "not sacred, unholy." An AFFABLE person is "easy to talk to," a PREFACE is "an introductory statement in a book." As a verb, to PREF-ACE is "to make an introductory statement." Finally FATE is from the Latin *fatum*, "what has been stated or ordained by the gods," although in Roman mythology sometimes the gods seem inferior to fate. From FATE we have FATALISM, "the belief that everything is fated," FATAL, originally "controlled by fate," now "deadly," and FATALITY, origi-nally "doomed by fate," now "a death due to an accident." Cognate with the Latin root *fa-* is the Greek root *pha-/phe-*, from which are derived PROPHET, PROPHETESS, PROPHECY, PROPHETIC, etc.

It is my hope that readers will find words so interesting that they will begin looking for roots, derivatives, and cognates and may even become readers of dictionaries!

J is for Jove.

JOVE is another name for JUPITER, king of the gods in Roman mythology and husband of Juno. From JOVE we get JOVIAL, meaning
"characterized by conviviality, happiness." (Jupiter was thought by
the Romans to be the source of happiness.) We also have JOVIAN
meaning "relating to Jove or Jupiter." From the root *Jov-* we get Jupiter, since Jove was the "father of gods and men." Note that in Latin
Juppiter has two *p*'s but in English only one. The last two syllables
of "Jupiter" obviously derive from *pater*, "father." The change of *a* in
pater to *i* in *Iuppiter* is due to what is called "vowel weakening" since
the accent was on the first syllable.

The Greeks called Jupiter *Zeus* (*pater*), that is, "Father Zeus."
In Old English the god of war and of the sky was *Tiu*, whose name
we have in TUESDAY. The Indo-European root **deiw-* also appears
in Latin as *deus*, "god," which gives us DEITY and, through French,
Adieu ("I commend you to God"). This root also gives us DIANA,
goddess of the moon and of the hunt. The Latin word for "day" is *dies*,
which also comes from this root, the fundamental meaning of which
is "bright." It seems, therefore, that the Greeks and Romans, or more
properly, their ancestors, the speakers of PIE, deified the bright sky
and worshipped it. *Dies* gives us DIARY ("a daily account") and DIAL
(from "sundial"). DIAL comes from Latin *dialis*, "daily," which consists of *di-*, the base of *dies*, "day," and the suffix *-alis*, "pertaining to."

Roman deities have also given us other words too. For example,
CEREAL is from Ceres, the goddess of agriculture. From Mars, the
god of war, we get MARTIAL, and from Mercury we get MERCURIAL,
meaning "changeable" or "volatile." The meanings of MARTIAL and
MERCURIAL have been influenced by astrology.

By Jove, the study of words and especially the etymology of words
sure is interesting!

K is for Kalends.

The *Latin Dictionary* of C. T. Lewis and C. Short says this regarding *k*: "K, k, was used in the oldest period of the language as a separate character for the sound k, while C was used for the sound g. In [the] course of time the character C came to be used also for the K sound and after the introduction of the character G, for that alone, and K disappeared almost entirely from the Latin orthography except at the beginning of a few words." (*Ortho-* here means "correct," and *-graphy* means "writing" and specifically "spelling.") *K* was used only for *Kalendae* and related words and at times for the African city *Karthago*.

Kalendae is derived from a root **kel-* meaning "to call." The first day of each month was called *Kalendae* because on that day "it was publicly announced on which days the Nones and Ides of that month would fall." The Roman calendar was extremely complicated when compared to ours because the Nones came eight days before the Ides, and the Ides fell on the thirteenth day of some months and on the fifteenth day of other months. Even so the calendar could and did get out of whack, and it was finally reformed by Julius Caesar in 45 BCE. His calendar, known as the Julian calendar, was in turn reformed in 1582 by Pope Gregory XIII. We use the Gregorian calendar today, and it is used across the western world, except for some branches of the Orthodox Church that still use the Julian calendar. We spell CALENDAR with a *c* instead of a *k* because the English borrowed the word, not from Latin, but from the French who used *c* instead of *k*.

I am sorry this is so convoluted, but some subjects, as is the case with life itself, can be very complicated.

L is for Luminescence.

Above under "C is for Convalescence" I discussed *-escence* and *-escent*, the first of which forms nouns, and the second adjectives. Both suffixes indicate "becoming or continuing some state." One Latin word for "light" is *lumen, lumin-*. The noun LUMINESCENCE, therefore, means "continuing to give off light." The adjective LUMINESCENT means "capable of exhibiting luminescence" (*AHD*). There is also LU-MINIFEROUS, which also means "giving off light" or "bearing light." A related Latin word for "light" is *lux, luc-*. Both *lumen* and *lux* derive from PIE **leuk-* (*e*-grade), **louk-* (*o*-grade), and **luk-* (zero-grade). From the *e*-grade we get *lux, luc-*, the most common Latin word for "light"; LUCULENT, "full of light"; LUCIFER (the "Light Bringer" hence the morning star, the devil as he was before his fall); *luna*, "the moon"; LUNAR, "having to do with the moon"; LUNACY, "intermittent insanity" (believed to be linked to the phases of the moon); LUNATIC, one so afflicted; and LUCUBRATE, a rare word that means "to work at night by lamplight." In Greek the word for "white" is *leukos* as in LEUKEMIA, a bone marrow disease that means etymologically "a condition (*-ia*) of white (*leuk-*) blood cells" (*-emia* from *-aemia*, from *haima*, the Greek word for "blood").

From the *o*-grade of this root (**louk-*) we have in English LUCID ("clear"), ELUCIDATE ("make clear"), and TRANSLUCENT ("permitting light to pass through").

I hope that readers are feeling enlightened.

M is for Multitudinous.

The suffix *-ous* means "full of" and "characterized by," as was mentioned above under "G is for Grandiloquence." It comes from Latin *-osus*, which also gives us English *-ose* as in VERBOSE, "full of words." MULTITUDINOUS thus means "full of multitudes." MULTITUDE in turn comes from *multi-* and *-tude*, the latter of which is a suffix that forms abstract nouns indicating a state or quality (e.g., SOLITUDE and FORTITUDE, "the state of being alone" and "the state of being brave," respectively). MULTITUDE, therefore, means "the quality of being numerous," hence "the people, the masses."

Mult- from Latin *multus*, "many," is found in numerous words (e.g., MULTICOLORED; MULTICULTURAL; MULTIETHNIC, a hybrid word being one-half Latin and one-half Greek—*ethnos* is Greek for "people"; MULTILATERAL; MULTILINGUAL; MULTIPRONGED; MULTITASKING; and MULTIVERSITY, a university with many campuses). Incidentally the *i* in MULTITUDE and many similar words is called a "thematic vowel"; it unites the base *mult-* to the suffix *-tude*.

Multus, meaning "much," brings to mind *magnus*, "large," as in MAGNANIMOUS. Etymologically this word means "having a large soul (*anima*) and mind (*animus*)." Currently it means "being generous in forgiving, noble." English has lots of words that are derived from *magnus* (masculine gender) and *magna* (feminine gender) including the latter in the phrase *magna cum laude*. As mentioned before, if you do well in college you may graduate *magna cum laude*. If you do extremely well, you may graduate *summa cum laude*, "with highest honors." If you do well but not unusually well, you may graduate *cum laude*.

MAGNANIMOUS means "great souled," and a *magnum opus* is a "great work" (i.e., a masterpiece). MAGNIFY means "to make larger." MAGNIFICENT means "splendid, excellent"; MAGNITUDE is parallel to "largeness," and a MAGNATE is "a powerful person."

I sincerely hope that all this talk about *mult-* and *magn-* is not too much for the "pusillanimous pussyfooters" as Spiro Agnew (US vice president, 1969–73) called the opponents of President Richard Nixon's Vietnam Policy. (PUSILLANIMOUS comes from *pusillus*, which is Latin for "weak.")

N is for Nationality.

The last principal part of the Latin verb "to give birth" is *natus,* from which we get such words as NATIVITY, NATAL, PRENATAL, POSTNA-TAL, and NATION. The last is "a group of people who share a country and have common customs, history, and originally common birth." The suffix -*ity* ("quality of, state of") forms abstract nouns.

To review and expand on something stated above under "E is for Eupeptic," this root originally began with *gn-* and has the forms (grades): **gen-, *gon-,* and **gn.* The first form is called the *e*-grade, the second the *o*-grade, and the last one the zero-grade, i.e., with no vowel. The last form loses the *g-* when it begins a word, but the *g-* shows up in PREGNANT ("before giving birth") and COGNATE ("born with"). (This root is not related to *genu-,* which means "knee" as in "genuflect.") The *e*-grade is found in GENE, GENDER, GENIUS, GENUINE, and GENERATION. The *o*-grade is found in GONAD ("reproductive gland") and EPIGONE ("born after," a "second-rate imitator" [*AHD*]). The zero-grade gives us BENIGN (Latin *benignus* = "well born"); MA-LIGN (Latin *malignus* = "evil-natured"); INNATE ("inborn"); and NOEL and *née* (from French). The word NAÏVE means "simple," "lacking in the ability to think critically" (i.e., like someone who has just been born). NAÏVE comes ultimately from Latin *nativus* through French *naïf.* The abstract noun from it is NAÏVETÉ. NATURE means "the outdoor world" including all living things and perhaps "all things that have been born." UNNATURAL is, of course, "contrary to nature," and PRETERNATURAL is "beyond nature but not quite above nature" (e.g., ghosts, zombies, and werewolves, also spelled werwolves), while SUPERNATURAL means "above nature."

O is for Obsequious.

The present stem of the Latin verb that means "to follow" is *seque-*, and the participial stem is *secut-*. The prefix *ob-*, which with assimilation can occur as *oc-*, *of-*, and *op-*, also has several meanings, such as "to," "for," "against," "in the way," and "hindering," or it may simply intensify the meaning of the root that follows. The dictionary defines OBSEQUIOUS as "showing servile deference," which means "showing slave-like submission."

To me obsequious suggests someone who follows you around for a definite reason: he or she wants something from you. A SEQUEL is "something that follows" (e.g., a movie or literary work that continues the story of a previous work). A SEQUENCE means "a series"; PROSECUTOR in a legal context suggests "one who is really going after you" (e.g., for breaking a law). The verb PROSECUTE, besides the legal meaning, means "to follow an undertaking until it is completed." To PERSECUTE, on the other hand, is "to oppress or harass someone" because of his or her race, religion, gender, or other identity.

Sometimes the *s* of this root may be disguised, as in EXECUTE (from *ec-* and *secut-*, where *c* and *s* combine to become *x*), meaning "to carry out," "make valid" (e.g., a will), and "to put to death." Other words from this root include CONSEQUENT, CONSEQUENCE, and CONSEQUENTIAL, the last of which means "important or influential." A SUITOR (from Latin *secutor* by way of French) is "one who courts a woman" or in law "a petitioner." Another form of this root is *sec-* giving us SECOND, which looks to me like an archaic participle meaning "following." Finally SECT ("a group of followers") is from *sectus*, an "archaic past participle" (*AHD*).

NON SEQUITUR means "it does not follow" and is a logical fallacy. It will be discussed in part three of this book under "N is for *Non sequitur.*"

SEGUE (via Italian) as a verb means "to move smoothly from one state, condition, situation, or element to another." All of these derivatives have the *e*-grade of the root. The *o*-grade is found in Latin *socius,* "a follower," "a companion," giving us SOCIAL and SOCIETY. The abbreviation SEQ. means "sequel," and SEQQ. means "the following things."

P is for Preposterous.

Something is PREPOSTEROUS if what should come afterward (*post-*, *posterus*) comes before (*pre-*). Such a situation is "absurd," that is, "illogical." (ABSURD, by the way, is from Latin *surdus*, which means "deaf." *Ab-* here intensifies the meaning of *surdus*. If something is absurd, you should turn a deaf ear to it.) We have plenty of words that begin with *pre-*, for example, PRENATAL ("before birth"), PRELIMINARY (before the *limen, liminis*, "the threshold"), PREJUDICE ("judging," i.e., forming an opinion, before learning the facts), PREFIX ("to attach before"), PREDECESSOR ("one who goes before"), PREDICATE (etymologically = "say before," but with several other obvious meanings), and finally two religious terms: PRELATE ("a high-ranking clergyman," "a bishop," "one who is carried before") and PRELAPSARIAN ("having to do with the time before the fall, the *lapsus*, of Adam and Eve"; compare COLLAPSE and RELAPSE).

One could give an equal number of words beginning with *post-*, which means "after." The -*post-* in the word PREPOSTEROUS has nothing to do with stakes, or army bases, or delivery of the mail. It is just plain "after," as in *post mortem*. POST BELLUM means "after the war"; other derivatives include POSTCOLONIAL ("after the colonial period in US history"), POSTEXILIC ("after the Babylonian captivity" in Jewish history), and POSTHASTE ("with great speed"). In music there are lots of PRELUDES, but only, as far as I know, a few POSTLUDES. POST-OP means "after the operation." We all know what PREPOSITIONS are, but according to the *AHD* there are also POSTPOSITIONS. The example given is "notwithstanding" in the phrase "these facts notwithstanding." Finally a story in a local newspaper recently reported that "A postmortem was done on the dog after he died." Does this sound funny to you? Could it be redundant? By the way, as in the word REDUNDANT, *red-* is used instead of *re-* before vowels. The Latin verb *undare* is from *unda*, "a wave," and it means "to surge." A good definition of REDUNDANT would be "superfluous," which also means "overflowing."

Q is for Quadrivium.

QUADRIVIUM in classical Latin meant "a place where four roads meet." In medieval Latin it referred to four of the seven subjects of the liberal arts curriculum, namely arithmetic, geometry, astronomy, and music. Before studying these subjects, however, one had to master the trivium, namely grammar, logic, and rhetoric. Although the traditional subjects are not usually given in this order, I think one should first master the language, then learn to think critically (identifying logical fallacies, etc.), and then finally give speeches.

QUADRIVIUM comes from *quadrus* (from *quartus* and ultimately *quattuor* meaning "four") and *via*, "way." TRIVIUM comes from *tri-*, meaning "three" and VIA ("way") and means "three ways." These seven subjects were known as the seven liberal arts. They were called "liberal" because the Romans thought it was the kind of education appropriate for a free (*liber*) person living in a free society. ("Liberal" in this context has nothing to do with politics.)

It is obvious that the Romans borrowed the idea of liberal arts education from the Greeks when we realize that the names of the seven subjects comprising the liberal arts curriculum are all from Greek. GRAMMAR is from Greek *gramma, grammat-,* "a letter of the alphabet." (ALPHABET, by the way, is also from Greek, *alpha* and *beta* being the first two letters of the Greek alphabet. Compare the way we talk about "the ABCs.") LOGIC is from *logike* (*techne*), "the art of reasoning" (*logos* = "word, reason"), and RHETORIC is from *rhetor,* "an orator." ARITHMETIC is from *arithmos,* "number." GEOMETRY is from *geometria* "land measuring," and ASTRONOMY is "the study of stars" (*astra*). MUSIC is from *musike* (*techne*), "the art of the Muses," the nine daughters of Zeus and Mnemosyne ("memory").

James V. Shall, a champion of liberal arts education and author of 30 books and 356 articles, says this about liberal arts education: "Any adequate concept of 'liberal arts' and 'liberal education' would, to be intellectually complete and honest, have to attend to the Greek and Roman classical traditions, to the Hebrew and Christian revelations, to the patristic and medieval experience, and finally to modern claims, especially those arising from science and politics."

I'm hoping all of this whets your appetite not only for a liberal arts education but also for the third section of this book, which deals with Latin phrases that are sometimes found in English. These phrases also contain words that give us English derivatives. Words derived from Latin are every bit as interesting as words derived from Greek. Of course, words derived from Anglo-Saxon are interesting too. In fact, for the LOGOPHILE ("lover of words") almost all words are interesting. One goal of this book is to make everyone who works through it a logophile.

R is for Reduce.

The Latin verb *duco, duct-* means "lead" and, because of the large number of English derivatives, it provides an excellent chance to re-view (or learn for the first time) quite a number of prefixes. The prefix *re-* means "back," "backward," and "again." Hence REDUCE means etymologically "lead back." ABDUCT means "to lead away," thus "to carry off by force," "kidnap"; the related noun is ABDUCTION. (By the way, the etymology of KIDNAP is just what you might expect: KID and NAP, an obsolete verb that meant "to steal.") ADDUCE, from *ad-* ("to" or "toward"), means to "lead to." (I shall give the etymo-logical meaning first for all these compounds of *duc-*.) CONDUCE or more commonly CONDUCIVE means "tending to lead to a certain re-sult." DEDUCE is therefore "to lead down" or "conclude," and EDUCE is "to lead out" (remember *e-* means the same as *ex-*). (Here there is an important point about EDUCATION; it should be "drawing out," not "pouring in," which is what INFUSION means!) Remember that there are two prefixes spelled *in-*. One means "in," "into," and "on" or "upon" as in INDUCE. The other *in-* is a negative and means "not" (e.g., INOPERATIVE).

Pro- means "in front of," "forth," as in PRODUCE, and *se-* means "apart," as in SEDUCE. There is also SUBDUCTION, a geological term that describes the forcing of one layer of earth under another. Finally there is INTRODUCE, which you know, and SUPERINDUCTION, a medi-cal and legal term meaning "to introduce as an addition."

Without a prefix there is DUCT, "a hollow passage through which a liquid flows" and DUCTILE, "capable of being drawn into wire."

There are a number of titles from this word (e.g., DUKE, DUCHESS, and DOGE, "a ruler in medieval Venice"). A DUCAT was a gold coin used in a DUCHY that was ruled by a duke or a duchess. Finally we should not forget that the Italians called Mussolini "*Il Duce*," which is from Latin *ducem*, "leader," minus the final *m*. *Führer*, the Germans' nickname for Hitler, means the same thing in German.

S is for Subliminal.

Sub- means "under," as is well known. It occurs as a prefix in many words and also sometimes in Latin phrases that are used in English such as SUBPOENA ("under penalty"), which is also used as a verb: "to subpoena someone." We also have SUB ROSA, which means "secretly, privately," from the practice of hanging a rose over the door of a secret meeting. SUBLIMINAL means "below the threshold of consciousness." *Limen, limin-* is the Latin word for "threshold." It is found in ELIMINATE, which is from *e-* and *limin-* ("to kick someone out over the threshold"). *Sub-* is found in many other words such as SUBMARINE (*mare* = "sea"), SUBTERRANEAN (*terra* = "earth"), and SUBLUNAR, "under the *luna*" (i.e., the moon). (Ancient peoples associated intermittent madness with the phases of the moon, hence LUNATIC.)

Sub- is also found in a few words derived from Greek such as SUBATOMIC (in Greek, *a-* means "not," *tom-* means "cut," and *-ic* means "pertaining to"). The ancient Greeks didn't know that atoms could be cut or split. This is also why they didn't have a word like SUBATOMIC or *HYPATOMIC (a word I coined that is parallel to subatomic but is pure Greek. Greek *hypo-* and Latin *sub-* both mean "under"). They thought nothing could be smaller than an atom. Notice too that the final *b* of *sub-* may be assimilated to (= "made like") the following consonant, as in "suffix" and "suggest."

The opposite of *sub-* is *super-* (also *supra-*), which is also found in many words such as SUPERSONIC (*son-* = "sound"), SUPERVISOR (*-visor* = "one who sees"), and SUPERINTENDENT. I am not sure what rule governs the use of *supra-* instead of *super-*, but two things are obvious from a glance in the *AHD*: There are only seven words listed that begin with *supra-*, and six of them have to do with anatomy (e.g., SUPRAGLOTTAL, "above the glottis," and SUPRAORBITAL, "above the orbit of the eye" [i.e., the eye socket]). Secondly, there are roughly eighty words that begin with *super-*!

To digress for a moment and introduce some Greek words, cognate with *sub-* is Greek *hypo-*, which also means "under" (as in HYPODERMIC), and cognate with *super-* is Greek *hyper-* (as in HYPERACTIVE).

There is also Greek *hemi-*, which is cognate with Latin *semi-*. Both mean "one-half." Remember, as explained above, cognate words are derived from PIE. *Super-* and *hyper-* are derived from PIE **uper*, which also gives us English "over." Also *sub-* and *hypo-* come from PIE **upo*, which gives us English "up." The origin of the initial *s* in Latin and *h* in Greek is, as scholars like to say, "obscure." In other words, no one knows where they came from! Remember too that items that begin with an asterisk are "hypothetical" forms; they have not been found in any manuscripts or inscriptions.

Back to Latin-derived words. SPECIES is from **spek-* "to look" and meant originally "the look, outward appearance" of something. Members of a species share the same "look."

Finally the Latin word *superbus* means "proud," "arrogant," but the English derivative SUPERB means "excellent." This is an example of a semantic change, which means a change in a word's meaning. We have had, on the other hand, many examples of phonetic changes (i.e., changes in sounds) but very few, if any, changes in meaning. It is impossible to cover everything in a *libellus* (Latin for "a small book").

T is for Turbulent.

TURBULENT means "violently disturbed." Etymologically it is "full of *turba*," which means "turmoil," "tumult," "a disorderly crowd." There is also PESTILENT ("full of pests," usually insects), VIRULENT ("full of viruses, poisons") VIOLENT ("full of *vis*, force"), OPULENT ("full of *ops, opis*, wealth, resources"), and SUCCULENT ("full of *succus*, juice"). These words are all adjectives. The noun-forming suffix is *-lence*. For each adjective there is a corresponding noun ending in *-lence* (e.g., TURBULENCE, PESTILENCE, VIOLENCE, OPULENCE.) The thematic vowel before *-lent* and *-lence* can be *u* or *i*; in VIOLENT it is *o*.

Corpus, corpor- is the Latin word for "body," hence CORPULENT and CORPULENCE. CORPUSCLE is from Latin *corpusculum*, which means "small body," *-culum* being a "diminutive" suffix. We also have CORPORAL, "pertaining to the body" (as in "corporal punishment") and CORPS, a division of the armed forces (via French), and CORPSE.

The suffix *-lent* has nothing to do with Lent, the period of penitence for Christians that comes between Ash Wednesday and Easter. This "Lent" is from Middle English *lente* ("spring") and Old English *lengten*, from the lengthening of the days in springtime. "Lent" is in fact related to "long," and for those who give up something for Lent (e.g., candy) it can indeed seem long.

U is for Unanimity.

The suffix *-ity* tells us that UNANIMITY is an abstract noun indicating "the state of being of one (*un-*) mind (*animus* in Latin)" (i.e., the state of being in complete agreement). There are two *un-* prefixes in English. One is from the Latin *unus* and means "one." It appears as *uni-*, as in UNICYCLE, unless the base of the word begins with a vowel, in which case it is *un-* as in UNANIMITY. The other *un-* means "not" or "the opposite of" as in UNATTACHED. *Uni-* meaning "one" is found in UNIFORM, UNIFY ("make one"), UNILATERAL ("involving only one side"; cf. BILATERAL and even QUINQUELATERAL, "five sides"), UNIVOCAL ("having one voice or meaning"), and UNICORN. CORN in unicorn is from Latin *cornu*, which means "horn" and gives us CORNET, CAPRICORN (the constellation resembles a goat's horn), and CARROT (from its horn shape). The English HORN is cognate with Latin *cornu* since both are derived from PIE **ker-* as in the Greek *-ceras*, which appears in the word RHINOCEROS ("nose horn"). From *rhino-* we also have RHINOLOGY, "the study of the nose," RHINOSCOPY, "the examination of the nose," and RHINITIS, "inflammation of the nose."

As stated above unanimity means "being of one mind" (*animus* in Latin). There is, however, a related word *anima*, which means "soul." *Anima* gives us ANIMAL ("alive, having a soul"); ANIMALCULE, "a very small animal" such as a bug; ANIMISM, which is "the belief in spirits that exist separately from bodies"; MAGNANIMOUS, "generous, courageous, having a big soul"; PUSILLANIMOUS, "cowardly, having a small soul"; EQUANIMITY, "level-headedness"; ANIMOSITY, which is "hostility," etymologically, "the state of being full of spirit"; and finally a verb, ANIMADVERT, "to notice" (i.e., to turn your mind to something). *Nota bene*: in my opinion there are cases where it is not clear if a word comes from *anima* or *animus*.

Both *anima* and *animus* are related to *anemos*, which means "wind" in Greek and gives us ANEMONE, also known as "windflower," and ANEMOMETER, "an instrument for measuring the speed of the wind."

V is for Vulpine.

VULPINE is from the Latin word for "fox," which is *vulpes*. Foxes have a reputation for being clever (cf. "foxy"); hence VULPINE means "clever and cunning." There are many kinds of foxes including "swift fox" (*vulpes velox*), "pale fox" (*vulpes pallida*), and "red fox" (*vulpes vulpes*). (Note that the scientific names for animals tend to be in Latin and Greek, e.g., *canis latrans*, "howling dog," is a coyote, and *felis domesticus* is a cat). A female fox is called a vixen.

The *AHD* gives the PIE word for "wolf" as *wlk^{w}o-. Among derivatives from it is WEREWOLF (also spelled "werwolf"). Compare the first syllable *were-/wer-* with Latin *vir* meaning "man" as in VIRILE and VIRTUE (which originally meant "manly").

A taboo deformation of *wlk^{w}o- is *lwk^{w}o-. "Taboo deformation" means that people considered it dangerous to utter the name of a feared animal; hence they would alter the name or use a euphemism. (A EUPHEMISM is "a kind or less offensive way of saying something," e.g., "they passed away" instead of "they died," "portly" instead of "fat." EUPHEMISM is derived from the Greek prefix *eu-*, "well" or "good," and *pheme*, "speech.") People who feared bears would refer to them as "the brown ones" or "the honey eaters." Hence *wlk^{w}o- was altered to *lwk^{w}o- by switching the first two sounds. The Romans then got *lupus*, "wolf," and we have LUPINE meaning "wolf-like." There is also a disease called LUPUS, the full name of which is lupus erythematosus (the latter word is from the Greek word for "red"). Remember that the vast majority of scientific and medical terms come from Latin and Greek. Now back to wolves. The PIE *lwk^{w}o- gave the Greeks *lykos*, "wolf," which gives us in English LYCANTHROPY, which is "the belief on the part of some mentally ill people that they are wolves!"

LYCOPODIUM is the name of a plant. The second part of the word comes from Greek *pous, podos* (base = *pod-* meaning "foot"). PODIUM means etymologically in Greek "small foot."

Who would have thought that WOLF, VULPINE, LUPUS, and the first part of LYCANTHROPY derived from the same PIE root? This is the fascinating kind of relationship you will discover if you study Latin and Greek and PIE roots!

Words Derived from
Latin Phrases

A is for *A posteriori.*

A posteriori means "from later," and its opposite *a priori* means "from before." Both phrases refer to ways people know truths. *A priori* knowledge does not depend on experience (e.g., knowing that "two plus two equal four" and that "bachelors are unmarried" are two examples of *a priori* knowledge). *A posteriori* knowledge, on the other hand, is justified by experience. In general, mathematical knowledge is *a priori,* but scientific knowledge is the result of experience and experimentation, and it is therefore *a posteriori.* Obviously the subject of how people know truths is more complicated than this, and anyone who knows anything about philosophy and philosophers knows that even such obvious matters as these can be challenged and debated.

Although used today mostly by philosophers, these terms first appeared in a Latin translation of Euclid's *Elements,* a treatise on geometry that was written ca. 300 BCE.

By the way, the number-two man in a monastery (just below the abbot) is often called the PRIOR. Likewise, in a convent the nun just below the abbess may be called the PRIORESS. The word "abbot" does not come from Latin or Greek but from Aramaic, a Semitic language, which is related to Hebrew.

Students of Latin know, and students who hope to take Latin someday should know, that *posterior* and *prior* are comparatives. Consider, for example, *altus* ("high"), *altior* ("higher"), and *altissimus* ("highest").

A fortiori is a similar phrase that comes to mind in this context. It means "for a stronger reason" (e.g., if three people cannot do a certain job, *a fortiori* two would not be able to do it).

There are a few other similar Latin phrases that are occasionally used in English (e.g., *ab origine,* which means "from the beginning"). (Notice that the preposition *a* becomes *ab* when the following word begins with a vowel.) *Ab ovo usque ad mala* means "from the egg to the apples" (i.e., from beginning to end). The typical Roman meal began with an egg dish and ended with apples. (The Latin word for "apple" has a long *a* and has nothing to do with *malus, mala, malum,* which means "bad.") Finally there is *ab urbe condita,* which means "from the founding of the city" and is abbreviated AUC. When giving dates the Romans counted the years from the founding of Rome as we use BCE and CE.

B is for *Beati pauperes spiritu: quoniam ipsorum est regnum caelorum.*

In Matthew 5 we have what are called the Beatitudes. Matthew gives nine of them; Luke has only four. Here we analyze two of them. The Beatitudes are a part of the Sermon on the Mount. *"Beati pauperes spiritu: quoniam ipsorum est regnum caelorum"* is the first beatitude in Matthew's gospel and means "Blessed are the poor in spirit, for theirs is the kingdom of Heaven." *Beatus* means "blessed," and here it is masculine plural because it must agree with *pauperes*, which is also masculine plural. From *beatus* we also get BEATIFIC, which means "characterized by great joy." There is also BEATIFY, which means "to declare that someone is a saint in Heaven." BEATITUDE itself is an abstract noun that means "supreme blessedness or happiness." (The common suffix *-tude* forms abstract nouns. Cf. FORTITUDE from *fortis*, "strong," and MAGNITUDE from *magnus*, "large.") *Spiritu* means "in or with respect to spirit." *Quoniam* is one of the Latin words that means "because" and *ipsorum* means "theirs." *Est* is the Latin word for "is." *Regnum* means "kingdom" and has the same root that is found in *rex* (which is from *reg-* and *-s*) meaning "king," *regina*, "queen," *regius*, "royal," and the verb *rego, regere*, which means "to rule." Finally *caelorum* is from *caelum*, which means "heaven" and gives us CELESTIAL, "heavenly," and the proper name CELESTE.

Another beatitude says *"Beati misericordes: quoniam ipsi misericordiam consequentur."* This can be translated as "Blessed are the merciful since they shall obtain mercy." *Miseri-* is from a verb that means "to have mercy, to pity" and *cor, cordis* meaning "heart." Note that here and in the beatitude in the previous paragraph the verb *sunt*, "are," is omitted, which is common in Latin. It has to be understood or supplied by the reader. Finally *consequentur* is the future of the verb *consequor*, which means etymologically "follow with," and then "overtake," and finally "obtain."

C is for *Cogito ergo sum.*

René Descartes (1596–1650), the famous French philosopher, was looking for a solid starting point and foundation for his philosophy. He therefore set out to doubt everything he could doubt in an attempt to find out if there was anything he couldn't doubt, i.e., if there was anything that was INDUBITABLE (a nice word that just means "cannot be doubted"—*in* = "not"; *dubit-* = "doubt"; *-able* = "able to"). Hence he suspended belief in everything in the universe including his body, God, the past, mathematical facts, etc. Descartes explains his project thus:

> But instantly I realized that, while I wanted to think that everything was false it was necessary that I who was thinking thus must be something. And I noticed that this truth: I think, therefore I exist was so solid and so certain that even the most extravagant speculations of the skeptics could not shake it. I concluded, therefore, that I could accept it without hesitation as the first principle of the philosophy I was seeking.
>
> *Discourse on Method*, Part Four, Rene Descartes
> (author's translation)

Descartes, then, set out to reestablish on the basis of this foundation the existence of everything he had doubted: his body, God, the universe, etc.

From *cogito* we get in English COGITATE, "to ponder," COGITATION, "serious thoughts," and EXCOGITATE, "to consider something carefully." *Ergo* meaning "therefore" is occasionally used in English, especially by people who have studied Latin.

Sum is the first person singular of the verb "to be" in Latin and means "I am." The present tense of this verb in Latin is *sum* (I am), *es* (you [singular] are), *est* (he, she, it is), *sumus* (we are), *estis* (you [plural] are), and *sunt* (they are). The root is **es-*. The *AHD* explains that the following words (plus others too) all come from **es-*: AM, IS,

YES, SOOTH, SOOTHE, ENTITY, ESSENCE, ABSENT, INTEREST, *ont-* as in ONTOLOGY ("the study of being"), and SWASTIKA (a sign of good luck in Sanskrit)!

Turning now to Greek derivatives from PIE *es-*, in the fourth century CE there was a great controversy among Christians debating the nature of Jesus. The controversy involved *homoousia* versus *homoiousia*. Homoousia means "the same in being" (*homo-* = "same") while homoiousia means "similar in being" (*homoi-* = "similar"). Arius (260–336 CE) was a Christian priest who was later declared a heretic; he claimed that Jesus was only similar in being with the Father. At the Council of Nicea in 325 CE, however, the Church declared that Jesus was "one in being" with the Father. The whole controversy was over one letter, the letter *iota*, the smallest letter in the Greek alphabet, which made the difference between *homo-* (same) and *homoi-* (similar).

This is the only section in this book that deals with ONTOLOGY, "the study of being," which is the most abstract part of philosophy.

D is for *Draco dormiens numquam titillandus.*

This means "a sleeping dragon is never to be tickled" or more freely "never tickle a sleeping dragon." This is the only saying in this book that is not from classical or medieval Latin. It is the motto of the Hogwarts School of Witchcraft and Wizardry in the Harry Potter books. This saying means the same as "Let sleeping dogs lie." The ancient Romans may never have known dragons as we know them. For them *draco* meant "serpent," probably a large scary one. Today *draco* is also a constellation that resembles a serpent. *Titillandus* is from the Latin verb *titillare*, "to tickle" or "titillate." Here it is a gerundive, which is a future passive participle. In *Draco dormiens numquam titillandus*, the word *est* has been omitted and must be supplied. Some Latin gerundives that are commonly found as English words are AGENDA, MEMORANDA, ADDENDA, and CORRIGENDA. All come from Latin neuter plurals and mean "things to be done," "things to be remembered," "things to be added," and "things to be corrected." You'll find these words everywhere. A REVEREND, by the way, is "a person to be revered," etymologically "to be feared," but perhaps today we would say "to be respected."

Dormiens, dormit- is from the Latin verb that means "to sleep." It gives us DORMANT ("sleeping") and DORMITORY ("a place for sleeping"). One of the meanings of *-ory* is "place for." *Numquam* is the opposite of *semper*, which means "always." The motto of the US Marine Corps is *semper fidelis* ("always faithful").

E is for *Ex abundantia cordis os loquitur.*

This quotation, which means "the mouth speaks from the abundance of the heart," is found in the New Testament twice (Matthew 12:34 and Luke 6:45). The Latin word for "heart" is *cor, cordis*, which gives us CORDIAL, that is, "warm and friendly." *Os, oris* means "mouth," from which we get "oral," "pertaining to the mouth." *Loquitur* is the third person singular of the verb *loquor, locutus*, which means "to speak," from which we get CIRCUMLOCUTION, ELOQUENT, SOLILOQUY, VEN-TRILOQUIST, and several other words.

There are many other Latin sayings that begin with *ex*, for example, *ex Africa semper aliquid novi*, which means "something new is always [coming] out of Africa." This Latin saying is a translation of a Greek proverb. Why the Greeks thought something new was always coming out of Africa isn't clear. (Reminder: in Latin the verb may sometimes be omitted.) *Ex amicitia pax* means "Peace from (or perhaps through) friendship." *Amicitia* is an abstract noun from *amicus*, "friend," and *pax* (*pacis*) gives us "pacific," "pacify," and "pacifist."

Ex libris means "from the books (of an individual)." Readers might want to put this before their names in their books. *Ex nihilo nihil fit* means "Nothing comes out of nothing." One can deduce from this that, if in the distant past at some time there was absolutely nothing, there wouldn't be anything today. *Fit* is from the irregular verb *fieri*, which is used for the passive voice of *facio, facere* "to make." *Ex officio* means "by virtue of one's office." For instance, the vice president of the United States is *ex officio* the president of the senate. *Ex tempore* means "from [this moment of] time" (i.e., without preparation, spontaneous). *Ex oriente lux* originally referred to the sun rising in the east but has been broadened to refer to cultural practices that come from the Orient, i.e., the part of the world that is to the east of Europe (though this use of "Orient" is now considered archaic). *Lux, lucis* is the Latin word for "light"; perhaps here it means enlightenment.

F is for *Felix qui potuit rerum cognoscere causas.*

A famous quotation is from Book II of the Roman poet Vergil's *Georgics* (line 490). (To digress for a moment from Latin to Greek, *Georgics* [and the name George] come from the Greek *ge* meaning "earth" and **werg-/*worg-* meaning "work," from which we get ERG, a unit of work, and the *-org-* of GEORGE, which means "farmer" [i.e., one who works the earth]). In the line *Felix qui potuit rerum cognoscere causas*, Vergil says, "Blessed is the person who has been able to understand the causes of things." Commentators are united in thinking that Vergil here is referring to the Roman poet Lucretius (ca. 97–55 BCE), who set forth the principles of the philosophy of Epicureanism in his poem *De Rerum Natura* ("On the Nature of Things"). Epicurus (341–270 BCE) was a materialistic philosopher who taught that the goal in life should be a peaceful, tranquil mind free from the fears of being punished in the afterlife. Vergil grants that the followers of Epicurus are *felix* (i.e., happy and blessed; cf. English "felicity"), but he understands that the person who has never studied philosophy but knows the rural gods Pan and Silvanus and the nymphs is also fortunate. The latter person (and no doubt Vergil too) appreciates the mystery and majesty of nature, which can be lost to the materialist who has reduced everything to atoms and chance, as the Epicureans did.

The Latin word for "cat" is *feles* (cf. English "feline"), which may be why "Felix" seems an appropriate name for a cat, although the words are not related. *Potuit* is the perfect tense of the verb *possum, posse, potui,* which means "to be able." (A POSSE is the group of people the sheriff "is able to" call upon in an emergency.) *Rerum* is from *res,* the Latin word for "thing" (cf. "real," "reify," and "reality"). *Cognoscere* is the present infinitive of *cognosco,* which means "to know." Compare, in fact, "know" and *gno-* (both from PIE **gno-*). Our word "cause" comes straight from the Latin *causa.*

Another famous phrase that has *felix* in it is *O felix culpa,* which means "O happy fault." This paradoxical phrase comes from a hymn that is sung on Easter Sunday. The idea is that the sin of Adam ("original sin") had a happy consequence since it brought Jesus as a savior.

G is for *Graecia capta ferum victorem cepit et artes intulit agresti Latio.*

Greece having been conquered (by the Romans) took captive its uncivilized conqueror and introduced the arts into rustic Latium (the area around Rome)." This was written by the Roman poet Horace (65 BCE–8 BCE). In 146 BCE the Romans had defeated the Greeks in the battle of Corinth, and Greece became a province of the Roman Empire. What Horace means, however, is that in spite of the Roman victory, it was Greek culture that captured (and captivated) the less civilized Romans. Many Romans fell in love with Greek poetry, comedy, tragedy, philosophy, history, rhetoric, science, mathematics, medicine, etc., which, if the Romans had them at all, were less highly developed. Wealthy Romans went to Greece to study, and they hired Greek tutors for their children. Many Romans mastered Greek and both wrote and spoke it well. "Love of Greek culture" is called PHILHELLENISM. It existed among the Romans, and it exists even today.

Graecia is the Latin word for "Greece," and *capta* is from the last principal part of the verb *capio, capere* ("to take, capture") and means "having been captured." *Ferum* is from the adjective *ferus, -a, -um*, which means "wild." It gives us FERAL, meaning "untamed," and also "ferocious" and "ferocity." *Victorem* is the accusative case (= English "objective" case) of *victor*. The *-em* tells us it is the direct object of the verb *cepit*, which is a past tense of *capio, capere* mentioned above under *capta*. *Artes* is the plural of *ars, artis*, which means "art." *Intulit* is the past tense of a very irregular Latin verb, viz. *infero, inferre, intuli*, which means "to carry in" or "introduce." *Agresti* is from an adjective *agrestis* (masculine and feminine), *agreste* (neuter) that modifies *Latio*, the area around Rome. The extent to which the Greeks were culturally superior to the Romans is, of course, a very controversial subject. Horace's use of the words *ferus, -a, -um* to describe the Roman conquerors and the word *agrestis, -e* to describe Latium makes it quite clear, in my opinion, that he was an admirer of Greek culture.

H is for *Homo doctus in se divitias semper habet.*

This sentence means "the educated person always has his riches within." The following fable illustrates this maxim:

> Simonides, who wrote outstanding poetry, in order to make his poverty easier to endure, began to visit the most renowned cities of Asia singing his praises of victors in games for a fee. After he became rich in this way, he developed a desire to sail home and visit his fatherland. He had been born on the Aegean island of Ceos. The ship that he boarded, being rather old, encountered a terrible storm and fell apart on the high seas. All grabbed their money and other valuables to help with their survival. A rather inquisitive guy said to Simonides, "Aren't you taking any of your valuables with you?" He replied, "All my valuables are within me." Only a few succeeded in swimming to shore; most drowned weighed down by their possessions. There were thieves on shore who robbed the survivors of what they possessed, leaving them completely naked. Fortunately the ancient city of Clazomene was close by, and so the survivors swam toward it. In the city there was a certain scholarly fellow who had read Simonides's verses for many years and was a great admirer of him. Having recognized him from his manner of speaking, he eagerly welcomed Simonides into his house and showered him with clothes, money, and servants. The other survivors were begging for food. When Simonides chanced upon them he said, "I carry all of my valuables within me. Everything you rescued you have lost."

> (author's translation)

This fable is by Phaedrus (ca. 15 BCE–ca. 50 CE), who was a well-educated slave from Thrace, in northern Greece, and became a freedman of the emperor Augustus. Little is known about Phaedrus, but more than five books of fables in verse have survived.

Doctus in the phrase *homo doctus* is the past participle of the verb *doceo, docere*, which means "to teach." Thus *homo doctus* is "a person who has been taught" (i.e., an educated person). *In se* means "in himself/herself." *Divitias* means "wealth" and is related to our word DIVINE, both coming from the root **dyeu-*, which means "to shine." Perhaps the meaning develops from "bright sky" to "divine" to "blessed" to "fortunate." (See **dyeu-* in Appendix I of the *AHD*.) *Habet* is from the Latin verb *habeo, habere* that means "to have." It means "has" here.

I is for *In hoc signo vinces.*

In 306 CE Constantine (later known as "the Great") was appointed deputy emperor of the western part of the Roman Empire by the emperor Galerius. As such he ruled over Britain and Gaul (modern France). Maxentius, who was Constantine's brother-in-law, attacked Galerius, defeated him, and seized Italy. When Galerius died in 311, Constantine invaded Italy and defeated Maxentius in a famous battle at the Milvian Bridge just outside Rome. Eusebius, a Christian historian, claims that Constantine told him that before the battle at the Milvian Bridge he saw a cross of light in the sky with the words "In this sign thou shalt conquer" in Greek above the sun. Translated into Latin the apparition became *In hoc signo vinces.* Constantine became a devout Christian as a result of this vision. In 313 CE he issued the "Edict of Milan," which outlawed persecution of Christians. In 325 he personally attended the Council of Nicea, a famous Christian gathering. He built many Christian churches including Santa Sophia in Byzantium, which was renamed Constantinople and is today known as Istanbul. When Constantine died in 337

"Christianity was well on the way to becoming the state religion of the Roman Empire" ("The Battle of the Milvian Bridge," Richard Cavendish, *History Today*, online).

   Hoc in this famous saying means "this." *Signo* is from *signum* and means "sign." *Vinces* is second person singular, future tense of the verb *vinco, vincere*, which means "conquer."

J is for *Jura novit curia.*

Jura novit curia means "The court knows the law." This legal principle means that lawyers in civil law cases don't have to explain the law to the judge; it is assumed that he or she knows the law. The lawyers must show how the law applies to their client in the particular case. *Jura* is the plural of *jus, juris,* which means "right," "law," and "justice." *Jura* is a neuter plural noun and could be either the subject or the direct object in this sentence. Since, however, *curia* can only be nominative singular, it has to be the subject, and *jura* must be the direct object. *Novit* means "he, she, or it knows." It is from an earlier **gnovit,* which is related to our word "know," both words being derived from PIE **gno-*. (Unlike us, when the Romans ceased to pronounce the initial *g,* they ceased to spell it too.) Among English words related to *jus, juris* are JURIDICAL, JURISDICTION, JURISPRUDENCE, JURIST, JUROR, JUST, and JUSTICE, all having to do with the law. (Notice that when the *s* of *jus* comes between vowels, it changes to *r.* This is called "rhoticism" from the Greek name for *rho,* which is equivalent to English *r.*) *Curia* comes into English unchanged. *Inter alia,* it refers to the central administration of the Catholic Church. The *AHD* says that *curia* is possibly from **co-vir-ia,* which means "men together." This shows that there were no women in the original Roman curia. Finally there is an important legal saying: *Ignorantia legis neminem excusat,* which means "Ignorance of the law excuses no one." Thus if hauled into court, don't think you will be found innocent by pleading, "I didn't know what I did was against the law!"

L is for *Lex Dei vitae lampas.*

Lex Dei (est) vitae lampas means "The law of God is the lamp of life."
It is the motto of the Presbyterian Ladies' College in Melbourne, Aus-
tralia. The base of the word *lex* is *leg-*, and from it we get such words
as LEGAL, LEGISLATOR, and PRIVILEGE (a "private law"). *Dei* is the
possessive case of *Deus,* "God," and means "of God." *Vitae* is the possessive case of *vita,* "life," and it means "of life." Finally *lampas* means
"lamp." Of special interest to people interested in etymology is the
possibility mentioned in the *AHD* that *leg-* meaning "law" may be
the same root that means "to collect," the legal meaning coming from
"a collection of laws." *Leg-* meaning "collect, gather" could then also
be the source of words whose meanings relate to "read" ("gather the
meaning"): LECTURE, LECTERN, LEGEND, LEGIBLE, INTELLIGENT,
and SELECT. Readers who find this interesting are urged to consult
*leg- in the *AHD*'s Appendix I: Indo-European Roots, where derivatives from the *o*-grade of this root (*log-*) are listed.

   Lex lata is "a law that has been passed." *Lex loci* means "the law of
the place." *Lex scripta* is "a law that has been written down" as opposed
to *lex non scripta,* "an unwritten law." Finally *lex parsimoniae* is the
"law of parsimony," which states that entities should not be multiplied
unnecessarily. This means that if there are several competing theories
or explanations, the simplest one is to be preferred. This rule is also
called "Ockham's razor" after William of Ockham (ca. 1285–1347),
an English Franciscan friar.

   Another short Latin *l* word is *lux,* which means "light." It appears in quite a number of Latin mottos and sayings. *Lux hominum
vita* means "light is the life of people." *Lux in tenebris lucet* means
"the light shines in the darkness." *Lux sit* means "let there be light"
(and there was light), which comes from Genesis 1:3. *Lux tua nos
ducat* means "let your light guide us." *Lux, veritas, virtus* (Light,
truth, virtue) is the motto of Northeastern University, and the motto of the University of North Dakota is *Lux et lex. Lux et veritas* is
the motto of several other institutions.

M is for *Mens sana in corpore sano.*

The famous Latin phrase *Mens sana in corpore sano* means "a sound mind in a sound body" or "a healthy mind in a healthy body." It occurs first in a work by the Roman poet Juvenal. Many athletic clubs, military groups, and educational institutions use it as their motto. *Mens, mentis* (base *ment-*) means "mind, thought" and it gives us MENTAL, MENTION, and MINERVA, the Roman goddess of wisdom. *Sana* means "sound," "healthy," "sane" and gives us such words as SANITY, SANITARIUM, and INSANE. *Corpus, corporis* (base *corpor-*) gives us CORPS, CORPSE, CORPUSCLE, CORPULENT, and several other words.

There are many other Latin sayings that begin with *m* such as *mea culpa, mea culpa, mea maxima culpa. Culpa* means "fault" and it gives us CULPABLE, CULPRIT, and EXCULPATE. *Maxima* is the superlative of *magnus, -a, -um* and means "largest," "greatest." Other Latin sayings that begin with *m* are *mirabile dictu* ("marvelous to relate") and *mirabile visu* ("marvelous to behold").

In English we have what are called "absolute constructions." They tend to come at the beginning of sentences and are "absolute" in the sense of being separated grammatically from the rest of the sentence (e.g., "All things being equal..." and "Barring bad weather..."). Latin has these also, and they are called "ablative absolutes." Two examples are *mutatis mutandis* and *mutato nomine.* The first one means "the things that have to be changed having been changed." The second one comes in the saying *mutato nomine, de te fabula narratur,* which is from the Roman poet Horace and means "the name having been changed, the story applies to you." *De* means "concerning." *Te* means "you." *Fabula* means "fable" or "story," and *narratur* means "is narrated" or "is told."

N is for *Non sequitur.*

Non sequitur means "It does not follow," and it is a logical fallacy. If one says "All men are mortal; Sam is a man; therefore Sam is mortal," we have a valid syllogism because all men are mortal; Sam belongs to the class of men, therefore *ipso facto* he belongs to the class of mortal beings. If, on the other hand, one says "Some athletes are swimmers; Betty is some athlete; therefore Betty is a swimmer," we have a *non sequitur* because "some" is used differently in the premises, which results in a faulty syllogism.

Besides the above phrase, there are a large number of Latin sayings that begin with *n*. Here are six that begin with *nemo* "nobody": *Nemo dat quod non habet,* "nobody gives what he does not have," which is self-evident. *Nemo est supra legem,* "nobody is above the law." *Nemo iudex in causa sua,* "no one [can be] the judge in his own case." *Nemo malus felix,* "no evil person [is] happy." *Nemo mortalium omnibus horis sapit,* "no mortal is wise all the time." *Nemo tenetur se ipsum accusare,* "no one is obliged to accuse himself."

Ne quid nimis means "nothing to excess" or more freely "all things in moderation." *Numen lumen* means "God is our light," which is the motto of the University of Wisconsin. (Note that *est* is omitted, as often happens.) *Nihil boni sine labore* means "nothing good [is achieved] without work." *Nihil humani mihi alienum* means "I am a human, nothing human is alien to me" (note that *est,* "is," must be understood by the reader). *Nihil sine labore,* the motto of various schools, means "Nothing without labor." *Nihil sine numine* is the motto of Colorado. Literally it means "nothing without the divine will." *Nomen est omen* means "[your] name is an omen" or "[the] name is an omen." *Non scholae sed vitae* means "not for school but for life" (i.e., "[you should learn] not for school but for life"). There is also *Non sibi sed patriae,* which can be translated "not for yourself but for the fatherland." Finally, a very famous saying is *nosce te ipsum,* "know thyself." This was inscribed on the Temple of Apollo at Delphi according to the Greek writer Pausanias.

O is for *Omnia vincit amor.*

Under the letter *r* we will discuss *repetitio est mater studiorum*, which means "repetition is the mother of studies." On this page we are demonstrating the truth of that saying. If students using this book remember anything at all, it should be the meaning of *omnia*, "all things." *Omnia vincit amor* means "love conquers all" and is from the poet Vergil. *Omnia cum Deo* means "all things with God." *Omnia mutantur; nihil interit* comes from the poet Ovid (43–17 BCE), and the phrase can be translated "all things change (but) nothing perishes." *Omnia omnibus* means "all things to all people." This was written by Saint Paul in 1 Corinthians 9:22 where he says he became all things to all people in order to save all. *Omnia praesumuntur legitime facta donec probetur in contrarium* is a legal saying that can be translated as "all things are presumed to be lawfully done, until the opposite is proven," something for which we should be very thankful. Another way of putting it could be "Innocent until proven guilty."

Omnis traductor (est) traditor means "Every translator is a traitor." This rather strong statement is especially true of poetry, in which case so much is "lost in translation." It is also said that "translation is the art of failure." It is because of this fact that many people study foreign and classical languages so they can read poetry in the original language. *Omnia opera* means "all the works." One might say for instance "I own the *omnia opera* of Shakespeare."

The phrase *omnium gatherum* is used occasionally to mean "miscellaneous collection" by people who are trying to be clever or funny. *Gatherum* is not a Latin word; rather, it is formed from the English word "gather" and the Latin ending *-um*.

P is for *Petitio principii.*

This is a subject I have wanted to discuss for years. *Petitio principii* is a logical fallacy that is usually translated as "begging the question" but would be better translated "assuming what needs to be proven." Here is an example: "Smoking causes cancer because smoke has carcinogens in it."

The first thing to get straight is that "to beg the question" never meant "to raise the question" until quite recently. Some people, in my opinion, wishing to sound learned began saying "beg the question" when all they meant was "raise the question." These people who apparently never studied logic wanted to sound learned, but all they did was show their ignorance. I am not the only person who is bothered by this misuse of the phrase. There is even a website set up by some people who want to educate the public regarding the proper meaning of *petitio principii*. It is begthequestion.info. They have T-shirts and mugs, and you can print out cards to distribute to those who misuse the phrase. (Hint: this is not a good way to make friends.)

A helpful discussion can be found in Mark Liberman's scholarly discussion entitled "Begging the Question: We have answers." The story starts with Aristotle, who listed "assuming the conclusion" as a logical fallacy. His Greek was translated in the Middle Ages as *petitio principii*, which came to be translated into English as "begging the question" when "assuming the conclusion" would have been much, much better. Unfortunately there are some scholars today who have given up and are urging that "beg the question" now be accepted because of its wide usage. The best advice comes from Liberman: use "assume the conclusion" or "raise the question." Never say "beg the question."

Q is for *Quo vadis?*

This phrase means "Whither goest thou?" In more modern English we would say "Where are you going?" According to the story, St. Peter was leaving Rome to escape the persecution of Christians under the emperor Nero (37–68 CE). On the road he encountered Jesus, and Peter said, "Lord, where are you going?" Jesus answered, "Back to Rome to be crucified again." This gave Peter the courage to return and resume his ministry. Eventually he was arrested and crucified upside down. There is a church in Rome called *Domine, Quo Vadis?* that commemorates this event. The story is not in the Bible, but in the apocryphal Acts of Peter. (APOCRYPHAL is an English word derived from Greek that means "of questionable authenticity.") In other words it may be a legend.

Per- as in PERSECUTION occurs in many English words (e.g., PERTINACIOUS, "holding on stubbornly," PERTURBATION, "being thoroughly agitated," and PERFECT, "having been done thoroughly"). Besides "thoroughly," *per-* can mean "very" and "to the bad," as in PERVERSION and PERJURY. PERVADE means etymologically "go throughout" (from *per-* and *vadere*, "to go" as in INVADE, EVADE, and *Quo vadis?*). PERSPICACITY is the ability to see through things, hence "acuteness of perception." *Perspicax* (base = *spicac-*) is Latin for "having penetrating eyesight."

PERSECUTION is from *per-* and *sequor, secut-*, which means "follow" and gives us a large number of derivatives (e.g., SECT, SEGUE, SEQUEL, SEQUENCE, CONSEQUENT, EXECUTE [*ek + secut-*], OBSEQUIOUS, SUBSEQUENT, and even SECOND).

R is for *Roma locuta, causa finita.*

This saying is attributed to St. Augustine (354–430 CE), who in a sermon is reported to have informed his flock that a certain controversial matter had been referred to the Pope, who ended the controversy with a definitive statement. The unabbreviated version would be *Roma locuta est, causa finita est.* ("Rome has spoken; the matter has been settled.") *Locuta est* is the perfect tense of *loquor* and means "has spoken." *Finita est* is the perfect tense of *finio, finire* and means "has been ended." Of course this saying could be easily used in any context. Suppose a legal matter is taken up by the Supreme Court, which issues a definitive ruling. People who know Latin could easily say, *Roma locuta, causa finita.*

The present tense of the verb *loquor* is found in the saying *Res ipsa loquitur,* which means "The thing speaks for itself." A woman, having had her appendix removed, goes to a doctor with stomach pains. An X-ray reveals that there is a scalpel in her stomach. "The case speaks for itself." The surgeon negligently left the scalpel behind!

Regnat populus means "the people rule" and is the motto of Arkansas. Notice that word order in Latin is freer than in English. This is because the role a word plays in a sentence in Latin is indicted by the ending the word has, not by the position of the word in the sentence.

Repetitio est mater studiorum means "repetition is the mother of studies." One has only to observe infants learning to walk, talk, feed themselves, and do everything else to realize the absolute necessity of repetition for mastering anything, from learning to play a sport or a musical instrument to learning to speak a foreign language or to read a classical language.

A final Latin saying that begins with *r: Res non verba,* "Deeds not words," (i.e., "actions speak louder than words"). Don't, however, take this to mean that words are not important!

S is for *Semper fidelis.*

Under the letter *r* we discussed *Repetitio est mater studiorum* and under *o* we had demonstrated the truth of the saying. On this page we are again illustrating the truth of that saying. *Semper fidelis* ("always faithful") is the name of a famous march composed by John Philip Sousa. It is considered the official march of the US Marine Corps. (By the way, FIDO is from *fidelis*; it means "faithful" and is a very good name for a dog.) *Semper fortis* ("always brave or strong") is an unofficial motto of the US Navy. *Fortis* gives us in English FORTITUDE and FORT. *Semper idem* means "always the same." Our words IDENTITY and IDENTIFY are derived from *idem*. *Semper invicta* can be translated "always invincible." (Rather freely one might say "never conquered.") *In-* means "not" and *victa* is from the Latin verb *vinco, vincere*, "to conquer." *Semper liber* means "always free." (By the way, *liber* meaning "free" has a long *i*. The word *liber* that means "book" has a short *i*.) *Semper paratus* means "always ready" or "always prepared," and it is the motto of the US Coast Guard (and also its official march). *Semper primus* means "always first" and is the motto of the 1st Infantry Regiment of the US Army. *Semper reformanda* (the full phrase is *Eccclesia semper reformanda est*) means "the Church is always in need of reformation." This saying was popular among certain Reformed Protestant theologians at the time of the Reformation, but it was also used by Catholic scholars at the time of the Second Vatican Council. Finally *semper sursum* is freely translated "always aim high" and is the motto of a number of schools. One may wonder about the etymology of *semper* itself. It is from the PIE root **sem-*[1], "one," "once," plus *per*, "during," "for," or "once and for all."

T is for *Timeo Danaos et dona ferentes.*

As the Roman poet Vergil tells the story in his epic poem the *Aeneid,* the Greeks attack Troy but are unable to breach the walls. Inspired by the goddess Athena, they build a huge wooden horse and hide within it a contingent of their best warriors. Pretending that the horse is an offering to the gods for a safe journey home, the Greeks sail to a nearby island and hide on the far side. Some Trojans think that the horse should be brought into the city; others, distrusting the Greeks, want to destroy it. While they are debating, Laocoön, a priest of Apollo, runs up urging them not to trust the Greeks: *Timeo Danaos et dona ferentes.* "I fear the Greeks," he says, "especially when they are giving gifts." With that he hurls a spear into the side of the horse. Then, as he conducts a sacrifice to the gods, two huge serpents come from the sea and kill him and his two sons. Taking this as proof that Laocoön was wrong, the Trojans breach their walls and drag the horse into the city. Late that night the Greek fleet returns, the warriors hiding in the horse are let out, and they destroy Troy. Laocoön's comment is the origin of the saying "Beware of Greeks bearing gifts."

From the PIE root *tim-* we have in English TIMID and TIMID-ITY. In mythology Danaus was the founder of Argos, an important Greek city. Vergil here uses *Danaos* to mean "the Greeks." *Donum* (plural *dona*) means "gift" and gives us DONATE. *Ferentes* is from *fero*, "to bear," "carry," and gives us INFER, DEFER, REFER, FERTILE, and FERTILITY.

Some other famous Latin phrases that begin with *t* are *tabula rasa*, *temet nosce*, and the logical fallacy *tu quoque*. *Tabula rasa* means "blank slate." More literally it means a tablet that has been erased. It is a translation of Aristotle's phrase *pinakis agraphos*, which means a tablet on which nothing has been written. (In Greek *a-* means "not" and *graphos* means "written.") Philosophers use this phrase to refer to the human mind before it has received any impressions from the senses.

Temet nosce means "know thyself." *Te* is the objective case of *tu*, which means "you" singular. The ending *-met* is defined in Latin dictionaries as a "pronominal suffix" and is equivalent to "self" in "myself," "yourself," etc. *Nosce* is the imperative singular of a verb that means "to know." "Know thyself" was inscribed on the Temple of Apollo at Delphi. When Thales, sometimes regarded as the first Greek philosopher, was asked what the most difficult thing is, he is reported to have said, "To know thyself." When asked what the easiest thing is, he replied, "To give advice." Sentiments similar to "Know thyself" are found in the most ancient traditions all over the world.

U is for *Ut biberent quoniam esse nollent.*

The ancient Romans believed that the will of the gods could be learned from birds by observing their flight patterns, position in the sky, cries, and eating patterns. This was called "taking the auspices" (from *au-*, which is from *avis*, "bird," and *specio*, "looking, watching"). When the Roman fleet went to sea, sacred chickens were taken along in cages. In 249 BCE the Roman fleet was preparing to attack the Carthaginian fleet, which was in port. Before attacking they had to ascertain the will of the gods by observing if the sacred chickens would eat. If they ate eagerly, it was a sign that the gods favored the Romans. The birds, however, refused to eat the grain they were served. Losing his patience, the admiral Publius Claudius Pulcher said *ut biberent quoniam esse nollent*, "since they won't eat, let them drink," and he threw them overboard into the sea! Because of the time spent with the chickens, the Romans lost the initiative and consequently the battle. Upon his return to Rome, Pulcher was court-martialed and exiled, his career being ruined. In the Latin, *nollent* means "they were unwilling"; *esse* with a long initial *e* is the infinitive of *edo*, "to eat." (Compare *esse*, the infinitive of the verb "to be," which has a short initial *e*.) *Biberent* is from *bibere*, "to drink," as in the English IMBIBE.

There is another famous story that involves taking the auspices. When Romulus and Remus were old enough to leave their hometown, Alba Longa, and found their own city, they set out in search of a good site. Eventually they came to a place where there were seven hills. Romulus thought that the Palatine Hill would be the best place; Remus disagreed and favored the Aventine Hill. To settle the disagreement they decided to "take the auspices" by observing the flight of birds to determine the will of the gods. Remus, stationed on his hill, observed six birds fly over. A minute later Romulus saw twelve birds fly over his hill. He claimed that he was the winner because of the number of birds. Remus claimed that he was the winner because birds flew over his hill first. The quarrel dragged on and finally Romulus decided to go ahead and begin construction. While the walls were being built, Remus jumped over them to show his contempt. This angered Romulus so much that he slew his brother and thereby became the founder of Rome.

V is for *Vade ad formicam, O piger, et considera vias eius, et disce sapientiam.*

A profound bit of wisdom comes from the book of Proverbs, which is in the Bible: *Vade ad formicam, O piger, et considera vias eius, et disce sapientiam.* It means "go to the ant, thou sluggard, consider its ways, and learn wisdom." If you've ever watched ants cutting leaves and transporting the pieces back to their nest, you will realize that they can teach us cooperation, perseverance, and diligence. There are even ants that keep aphids just as humans keep cows. The aphids produce a sugary honeydew that the ants love. The ants in turn protect the aphids from predators and will sometimes transport them to new nests. Other ants use the leaves they have taken to their nests to grow fungus that they eat.

Vade is from the Latin verb *vado, vadere, vas-* "to go." We have in English INVADE, INVASION, and INVASIVE, EVADE, EVASION, and EVASIVE, and PERVADE and PERVASIVE. This verb also appears in the famous phrase *quo vadis*, which we had above under "Q is for *Quo Vadis*." In the New Testament (Mark 8:33) Jesus says to Peter, *Vade retro me, Satana!*, which means "Get thee behind me, Satan!" A *vade mecum* is an item one carries around constantly, especially a book. It's a "constant companion." (Note that with certain words *cum* is appended to the word rather than coming before it as we would expect. Thus Latin uses *mecum, tecum, secum, nobiscum, vobiscum, quocum,* and *quibuscum* instead of *cum me, cum te, cum nobis,* etc., as we speakers of English would expect.)

FORMIC acid, by the way, occurs naturally in ants (*formica*), hence its name. The plastic Formica, on the other hand, is a trademark and has nothing to do with ants. From the Latin word *sapientia* we get the word SAPIENTIAL, and the word *sapiens* in the phrase *Homo sapiens* is related to it.

Considera is from *con-* and *sidera*, which means "stars." The verb CONSIDER may go back to the ancient practice of looking at the stars for navigation or to predict the future.

List of References

American Heritage Dictionary of the English Language. 5th ed. Boston/New York: Houghton Mifflin, Harcourt, 2011.

Burris, E. E., and L. Casson. *Latin and Greek in Current Use.* New York: Prentice Hall, 1949.

Ciardi, John. "Manner of Speaking." *Saturday Review* 55, March 11, 1972, 14.

Neruda, Pablo. *Memoirs.* Translated by Hardie St. Martin. New York: Farrar, Straus and Giroux, 1977.

Oxford Classical Dictionary. 4th ed. Edited by Simon Hornblower, Anthony Spawforth, and Esther Eidinow. Oxford: Oxford University Press, 2012.

Steiner, George. *After Babel.* Oxford: Oxford University Press, 1975.

Wheelock, Frederic M. *Wheelock's Latin.* 7th ed. New York: HarperCollins, 2011.

Appendix:
Principal Parts of
Latin Verbs

Latin verbs appear in many different forms depending on their use in a sentence. Thus, the same Latin verb may appear in different roots in English derivatives whose meanings are related. Learning which roots come from the same Latin verb is an effective way to increase one's English vocabulary.

Latin verbs fall into four groups called "conjugations." In addition there are irregular verbs such as the verb *sum, esse, fui, futurus*, "to be," which may have only one, two, or three principal parts, and do not belong to a conjugation; there are also deponent verbs, which have passive forms but active meanings and have three principal parts. Verbs in the first conjugation have principal parts like *amo, amare, amavi, amatus* that have *–o* as the end of the first principal part and *–are* as the end of the second principal part. Verbs of the second conjugation are like *doceo, docere, docui, doctus* and have *–eo* as the end of the first principal part and *–ere* as the end of the second principal part. Many verbs in the third conjugation are similar to *pono, ponere, posui, positus* and have *–o* as the end of the first principal part and *–ere* as the end of the second principal part. In the fourth conjugation the first principal part ends in *–io* and the second principal part ends in *–ire*; *audio, audire, audivi, auditus* is an example of a regular fourth conjugation verb. English words that are derived from Latin verbs tend to come from the second principal part or the fourth. In general we present verbs as they are found in *Wheelock's Latin* by Frederic M. Wheelock.

Greek verbs have six principal parts, but English derivatives tend to come from the first principal part. For that reason we do not give a list of the Greek principal parts, and in the Words Derived from Greek section we do not give all the principal parts of Greek verb but only the first one.

First conjugation

accuso, accusare, accusavi, accusatus

considero, considerare, consideravi, consideratus

do, dare, dedi, datus

excuso, excusare, excusavi, excusatus

muto, mutare, mutavi, mutatus

narro, narrare, narravi, narratus

praesumo, praesumare, praesumavi, praesumatus

reformo, reformare, reformavi, reformatus

regno, regnare, regnavi, regnatus

titillo, titillare, titillavi, titillatus

Second conjugation

deleo, delere, delevi, deletus

doceo, docere, docui, doctus

habeo, habere, habui, habitus

timeo, timere, timui

video, videre, vidi, visus

Third conjugation

bibo, bibere, bibi

capio, capere, cepi, captus

cognosco, cognoscere, cognovi, cognitus

dico, dicere, dixi, dictus

disco, discere, didici

edo, edere, (esse), edi, esus

facio, facere, feci, factus

nosco, noscere, novi, notus

praesumo, praesumere, praesumpsi, praesumptus

rego, regere, rexi, rectus

sapio, sapere, sapivi

specio, specere, spexi, spectus

vado, vadere, vasi

vinco, vincere, vici, victus

Fourth conjugation

dormio, dormire, dormivi, dormitus

finio, finire, finivi, finitus

intereo, interire, interivi, interitus

Deponent verbs

consequor, consequi, consecutus sum

loquor, loqui, locutus sum

sequor, sequi, secutus sum

Irregular verbs

fero, ferre, tuli, latus

fio, fieri, factus sum

infero, inferre, intuli, illatus

nolo, nolle, nolui

possum, posse, potui

sum, esse, fui, futurus

List of Prefixes and Suffixes

Greek Prefixes

a-, an-	without, not
ana-, an-	up, back, again, according to
anti-, ant-	against
apo-, ap-	away from, without, not
cata-, cat-, kata-, kat-	down, thoroughly
dia-, di-	through, across, between
dys-	bad, abnormal, impaired
ek-, ex-	outside of, away from, former
epi-	on, around, after
eu-	good, well
hyper-	above, beyond, exceedingly
hypo-, hyp-	below, under
meta-, met-	after, following, change
para-, par-	beside, alongside, beyond, abnormal, assistant
peri-	around
pro-	before
syn-, sym-	together, same

Greek Suffixes

-emia	blood
-ia	*forms abstract nouns*
-ic	of, relating to, pertaining to
-isk	*forms diminutives*

-ism	doctrine, theory, belief
-logue	speech, dialogue
-oid	resembling, related to, shaped like
-ol	a type of alcohol
-opsis	glimpse of
-osis	condition, act, process
-sis	act of, action, condition, process, state of, result of

Latin Prefixes

ab-	away from
ad-	to, toward
ante-	before, in front of
con-, com-, co-, cor-, col-	with
de-	from, down, away, reversal, undoing
dis-, di-, dif-	not, apart
ex-, e-	out of, away from, former
in-, il-, im-	not; in, into, on, upon
mal-	bad
ob-	against
per-	thoroughly, very, throughout
pre-	before
pro-	in front of, forth
re-	back, backward, again
se-	apart
sub-	under
super-	above, beyond, exceedingly
un-, uni-	one; not, opposite of

Latin Suffixes

-able	capable of, worthy of
-al	pertaining to
-esce, -escence, -escent	beginning, becoming; *forms inceptive words*
-ic	pertaining to, of
-ion	action, state of being, result of an action
-itude	*forms abstract nouns*
-ity	quality of, state of; *forms abstract nouns*
-lence	*forms nouns*
-lent	*forms adjectives*
-or	a person who does something
-ory	place for
-ose, -ous	full of
-tude	*forms abstract nouns indicating a state or quality*

Index of Words
Derived from Greek

Index of Words Derived from Latin